Bruce Mason is the most significant playwright in New Zealand's theatrical history. Of his more than thirty plays several have become classics, including *The Pōhutukawa Tree*. In 1977 he was awarded an Honorary Doctorate of Literature by Victoria University.

In 1980 he was made a CBE, and in 1982 he was given the New Zealand Literary Fund Award for Achievement.

Bruce Mason died in 1983.

The THW Classics collection
celebrates more than half a century of stellar publishing
at Te Herenga Waka—Victoria University of Wellington

The End of the Golden Weather by Bruce Mason *1962*
Ngā Uruora by Geoff Park *1995*
Breakwater by Kate Duignan *2001*
Lifted by Bill Manhire *2005*
Girls High by Barbara Anderson *1990*
Portrait of the Artist's Wife by Barbara Anderson *1992*
Wednesday to Come Trilogy by Renée *1985, 1986, 1991*
In Fifteen Minutes You Can Say a Lot by Greville Texidor *1987*
Eileen Duggan: Selected Poems edited by Peter Whiteford *1994*
Denis Glover: Selected Poems edited by Bill Manhire *1995*
The Vintner's Luck by Elizabeth Knox *1998*
Man Alone by John Mulgan edited by Peter Whiteford *1935*
Six by Six: Short Stories by New Zealand's Best Writers
            edited by Bill Manhire *1989*
Wild Dogs Under My Skirt by Tusiata Avia *2004*
A.R.D. Fairburn: Selected Poems edited by Mac Jackson *1995*
R.A.K. Mason: Collected Poems edited by Allen Curnow *1962*
Ursula Bethell: Collected Poems edited by Vincent O'Sullivan *1985*
Dick Seddon's Great Dive and other stories by Ian Wedde *1981*
Lost Possessions by Keri Hulme *1985*
Te Kaihau | The Windeater by Keri Hulme *1986*
The Pōhutukawa Tree by Bruce Mason *1960*
Hera Lindsay Bird by Hera Lindsay Bird *2016*
Gifted by Patrick Evans *2010*

The Pōhutukawa Tree

Bruce Mason

TE HERENGA WAKA
UNIVERSITY PRESS

Te Herenga Waka University Press
Victoria University of Wellington
PO Box 600, Wellington
New Zealand
teherengawakapress.co.nz

Permission to perform this play must be obtained from
Playmarket, PO Box 9767, Courtenay Place, Wellington,
New Zealand. The publishers acknowledge the assistance
and advice of Playmarket, which was established in 1973
to provide services for New Zealand playwrights.

A catalogue record for this book is available from the National Library
of New Zealand.

Cover design by Graham Percy (1960)
Printed by Blue Star, Wellington

Ngā mihi me taku aroha ki te iwi Māori

Note to the second edition

That the printed text of a New Zealand play demands a second edition is highly gratifying to an author. Since its publication in 1960, *The Pōhutukawa Tree* has been produced in Feilding, Gisborne, Taupō, Murupara, Ardmore (Teachers' College), Dunedin and improbably (though it seems, successfully) in Llangefni, Anglesey, Wales. Numerous societies have given private readings of the play, many with Māori actors in the leading parts, some taking the stage for the first time. The disinclination of Māoris to project themselves into another character has often prevented productions of the play; there are encouraging signs that this inhibition is losing its hold.

The play has also been translated into Russian but so far, prevented from production by what the translator is pleased to call the author's 'anti-Māori grimace' in the last act. This I don't profess to understand.

In Dunedin, in March–April 1963, the Southern Comedy Players offered me professional resources to direct the play and a highly experienced cast which included Elizabeth Murchie as Aroha Mataira who confirmed and extended the distinguished impression she made in the radio version of 1960. The cast of this production appears below.

As a result of directing the Dunedin season, I have made minor amendments to the text, amounting mostly to reduction of some over-explicit speeches. James Bertram in his friendly review of the printed text in *Landfall 59*, September 1961, observed that 'the reader may be put off by a set of stage directions which often try too hard, which read sometimes like a tourist brochure or a producer's peptalk to a sluggish cast.' I protest that I was concerned simply to fill out visual details but I bow to his judgement: stage directions in this edition are minimal.

B.M.
1963

Some Productions

New Zealand Players Theatre Workshop, Wellington, 1957

Queenie Mataira	Mary Nimmo
Roy McDowell	Paul Skinner
Rev. Athol Sedgwick	Ronald Lynn
Aroha Mataira	Hira Tauwhare
Johnny Mataira	Maia Sullivan
Mrs Atkinson	Helen Brew
Mr Atkinson	Frank Gawn
Sylvia Atkinson	Marie Collett
George Rawlings	William Campion
Dr Lomas	Bruce Mason
Claude Johnson	L. Assheton Harbord
Mrs Johnson	Mollie Marriott
Sergeant Robinson	Roger Tristram

Designed by David and Joan de Bethel and produced by Richard Campion and the author.
The cast was the same for the Auckland season, except that Charles Walker played Mr Atkinson, and James Healey, Claude Johnson.

BBC Television, 1959

Queenie Mataira	Hermione Gregory
Roy McDowell	Noel Trevarthen
Rev. Athol Sedgwick	Philip Latham
Aroha Mataira	Hira Tauwhare
Johnny Mataira	Norman Florence
Mrs Atkinson	Madge Ryan
Mr Atkinson	Redmond Phillips

Sylvia Atkinson	Bridget Armstrong
George Rawlings	Terence Bayler
Dr Lomas	Newton Blick
Claude Johnson	Lloyd Lamble
Mrs Johnson	Lesley Jackson
Sergeant Robinson	Jerold Wells

Designed by Richard Wilmot and produced by John Jacobs.

New Zealand Broadcasting Service, 1960

Queenie Mataira	Hiria Moffat
Roy McDowell	Alan Jervis
Rev. Athol Sedgwick	Antony Groser
Aroha Mataira	Elizabeth Rehu
Johnny Mataira	Ian MacIntosh
Mrs Atkinson	Linda Hastings
Mr Atkinson	William Austin
Sylvia Atkinson	Paddy Turner
George Rawlings	Grant Tilley
Dr Lomas	Basil Clarke
Claude Johnson	Selwyn Toogood
Mrs Johnson	Sinclair Ronald
Sergeant Robinson	Tim Eliott

Produced by William Austin.

Southern Comedy Players, Dunedin, 1963

Queenie Mataira	Elizabeth Booth
Roy McDowell	Richard Manning
Rev. Athol Sedgwick	Bruce Mason, Bernard Esquilant
Aroha Mataira	Elizabeth Murchie
Johnny Mataira	William Menlove
Mrs Atkinson	Katrena Speight
Sylvia Atkinson	Dallas Campbell
Clive Atkinson	Lindsay Campbell

George Rawlings	Robert Nisbet
Dr Lomas	John Blumsky
Claude Johnson	Bernard Hill
Mrs Johnson	Joan Metcalfe
Sergeant Robinson	Les Milnes
Wedding Guests	Meryl Faris, Gay McInnes, Pauline Young, Tony McNally, Philip Woollaston
Two Māori Women	Emma Grooby, Daisy Parata

Designed by Frank Grayson and directed by the author.

Act One

Scene One

The porch of the Mataira house. A large pōhutukawa tree in bloom hangs over the porch. It is a year or two after the Second World War. Sitting on the porch is Queenie Mataira, a comely-looking girl of seventeen. At her feet is a basket of pipis and rock mussels which she is splitting deftly but without enthusiasm. Behind her, a portable gramophone and a stack of old records. The gramophone is grinding out 'Moonlight Becomes You', sung by Bing Crosby, his voice badly eroded by steel needles.

Roy McDowell comes in from the bush at the back, quietly. He is a lithe young man dressed in T-shirt and jeans. He carries a towel and swimming trunks. He looks at Queenie, pauses, then creeps along the porch to the gramophone and takes the arm off the record. Queenie wheels round and they stare at each other.

Queenie: Who are you?

Roy: Roy McDowell. I know who you are.

Queenie: Who am I, then?

Roy: Queenie Mataira.

Queenie: How do you know that?

Roy: Te Parenga's not such a big place. You hear things.

Queenie: (*after a pause*) What do you want?

Roy: (*with insolent charm*) I'm lost.

Queenie: Lost?

Roy: Yeh. Went for a swim. Beauty, too. Thought I'd take a
                  short cut back to the pub. Found myself in the middle
                  of the bush. Never knew there was so much bush left
                  here! And now, well . . . I'm lost. (*He smiles at her,
                  winningly.*)

Queenie: (*coldly*) If you follow that path there, you'll come to
                  the road. Then it's straight on up to the pub. Better
                  get going.

Roy: What's the hurry?

Queenie: Listen: I'm by myself. My Ma; she don't like me to
                  have young men about.

Roy: Then your Ma better grow up.

Queenie: What do you mean?

Roy: Young men'll soon be about, baby.

Queenie: Don't you call me baby! I don't know you . . . Think
                  so?

Roy: You've got something.

Queenie: (*warily, but curious*) What've I got?

Roy: You want me to tell you? (*He sits beside her.*)

Queenie: Here! Who said you could sit down? Bit cheeky, aren't
                  you?

Roy: Give me a chance, I'll be more than cheeky.

Queenie: I'll give you no chance. Don't like cheek. Listen: my
                  Ma; she's told me about boys like you.

Roy: What she say?

Queenie: (*severely*) Give them a wide berth. That's what she say.

Roy: Don't like the sound of your Ma.

Queenie: She's fine woman. Good mother, too. I love her.

Roy: Good on you. I like mine, too . . . Here: can I help?

He takes a few shellfish from the pot, knife from his back pocket and begins opening the shells and emptying the fish into the pot. Queenie looks at him carefully.

Queenie: You staying at the pub?

Roy: No, working. In the bar.

Queenie: Oh. Where you from?

Roy: Waikato.

Queenie: You a barman there too?

Roy: Nah. My Dad's a grocer. Been working with him, four years now. Well, the old man and me: we had a bust-up, see. And he says, pack your bags; come back when you can behave yourself. So, here I am. Working holiday.

Queenie: You going to behave yourself?

Roy: (*slyly*) Don't know yet. See, eh?

Queenie: Why you come to Te Parenga? Nothing here.

Roy: I'll keep my eyes open.

Queenie: Listen: this is a dead hole. No one comes here.

Roy: Then they should. Beauty beach. Lots of sun. That's a start, isn't it?

Queenie rises, confused, moves off a few steps. Roy gives her a practised look; is satisfied with progress.

Queenie: What else you heard about me?

Roy: Only Māori family left here. Your father was a preacher: dead ten years ago. You all work on Atkinson's orchard. Your Ma does the garden; your brother Johnny prunes and picks; you grade and pack. You're seventeen, your brother's eighteen. How's that?

Queenie: You hear all this at the pub?

Roy: No. From Johnny.

Queenie: My brother Johnny?

Roy: Yeh. Picked him up on my bike last night.

Queenie: So that's why you're here!

Roy: Took him in for a drink.

Queenie: Johnny never drinks!

Roy: Yeh? Well, he's broken his duck, then. Liked it, too.

Queenie: Gee. Better not let Ma know. She hates liquor.

Roy: He a bit soft, your brother?

Queenie: No, he's all right. Why?

Roy: He reads kids' books. Robin Hood. He told me. And he's got a book full of drawings, too. All of Robin Hood.

Queenie: Has he? Funny; he never showed them to me.

Roy: (*moving towards her*) Well, I guess you're too young . . .

She slips past him, sits down, glances at him shyly and begins shelling vigorously. Roy moves slowly back to the porch, not taking his eyes off her, picks up the pile of records.

Roy: Where'd you pick up all this junk?

Queenie: Yeh: pretty old, aren't they? Sylvia Atkinson.

Roy: Oh. That's the girl getting married tomorrow, isn't it?

Queenie: Yeh. Great day, too. We're all going.

Roy: You going? How come?

Queenie: Listen, my Ma; she's worked there seventeen years. Does the garden. Great big garden, too. Full of rock pools and fountains and begonia houses. And Johnny: he runs the orchard, two years now. We make a lot of money for old Mr Atkinson. So why shouldn't we go to the wedding? We're like their own family.

Roy: Okay, okay.

Queenie: Look, you want to see the invitation? It's got a crinkly
            edge with gold on it.

Roy: No, skip it. I'll see you there, anyway.

Queenie: (*startled*) You going? You know the Atkinsons?

Roy: Will do, tomorrow.

Queenie: But how—

Roy: (*putting the records down*) No questions: no lies.

            *He sits down beside her, puts his hand on her knee. She
            looks at it uncertainly, then back at him.*

Queenie: Listen—

Roy: (*softly*) Anyone ever tell you what you look like?

Queenie: Yeh. My Ma does. Take that lipstick off, she says. You
            look cheap.

Roy: Your Ma's a bit cracked.

Queenie: Why?

Roy: Because, as Māori sheilas go, you're pretty hot stuff.

            *Queenie lunges at him so suddenly that he is pushed off
            the porch.*

Queenie: Don't you call me Māori sheila!

Roy: Easy! Easy!

Queenie: (*raging*) You cheeky Pākehā! Get out! Go on! Don't
            want you here.

            *Her eyes flashing, she gathers her fish, basket and pot
            together.*

Roy: (*contrite*) Sorry, Queenie.

Queenie: Go away. (*She walks along the porch to the door.*)
            Listen: my Ma, she's the leader of Ngāti-Raukura;
            everyone looks up to her. And my great-grandfather,

Whetumarama: he was a great chief. Took on the Governor and came out best. He threw the white man right out of Te Parenga. Great battle here. And we won. So now you get out too, Pākehā. On your way. (*She goes inside and the door bangs after her.*)

Roy looks after her, smiles, creeps over to the porch, picks out a record and puts it on. It is a very old war-time recording of 'In the Mood'. (Glenn Miller, if possible.) He stands back, clicking his fingers. Queenie appears at the window.

Queenie: You still here!

Roy begins to dance to the music. He is transformed by it, lithe and sinewy.

Roy: I'm gettin' hep, hep, hep! Come on outside!

Queenie: By golly, you cheeky. Cheekiest Pākehā I ever met. (*She opens the door and stands, watching him.*)

Roy: Come on! Get in the groove!

Queenie: Don't know how.

Roy: Teach you, then. Come on down!

Uncertainly, Queenie walks down to him. They go into a preliminary shuffle. She is at first a little stiff and awkward. Then the rhythm of the music seems suddenly to go right through her.

Roy: (*admiringly*) Gee. You're a natural.

Queenie: First time I ever danced with anyone.

Roy: Don't they have dances here?

Queenie: Twenty miles away. But Ma wouldn't let me go. Have a fit, eh.

The record locks on a scratch.

(*Very disappointed*) Ooh! (*She runs to take it off, looks at Roy, radiant.*) Gee, that was great.

Roy: So now do you want to see me again?

Queenie: (*after a pause*) Will you really be at the wedding?

Roy: See for yourself.

Queenie: Tell you then.

Roy: It's a deal. (*He picks up his towel and trunks.*) Well, mustn't miss my tea. I'd better be going.

Queenie: Look, if you take that path there, you won't meet Ma. It's a little longer, but it brings you out at the same place.

Roy: Okay, then. Hooray, Queenie.

Queenie: (*walking up with him, softly*) Hooray, Roy.

                  He goes off. Queenie turns back towards the house, smiling, humming. Then runs back.

Queenie: Roy!

Roy: (*off*) Yeh?

Queenie: Could we try the record again?

Roy: (*appearing*) Bit of a risk, isn't it?

Queenie: (*eagerly*) No, it's all right. Let's.

Roy: (*looking at her carefully*) Well, if you don't mind taking risks, Queenie ...

                  He puts on the record and Queenie comes close to him. She is already quite expert and noticeably more relaxed. They dance for a few seconds and the Reverend Athol Sedgwick enters, quietly. English, earnest, humane. Roy sees him at once and stops dancing. Queenie, impervious, does a dazzling turn and finds him looking at her. She stops, confused, then runs and turns the gramophone off.

Sedgwick: (*smiling*) Good afternoon.

Queenie: Hello.

Roy: Gidday.

Queenie: (*nervously*) Better go now, Roy. Time for tea, eh.
                Almost.

Roy: (*moving off*) Yeh. Well, so long, Queenie. Don't forget
                now: tomorrow, eh? You promised.

Queenie: (*hurriedly*) Okay. Hooray, then.

Roy: (*disappearing*) Hooray, Queenie.

Sedgwick: Friend of yours?

Queenie: No I just met him.

Sedgwick: He works at the pub, doesn't he?

Queenie: Yes. He got lost, on his way back from the beach.

Sedgwick: (*finding this charmingly transparent*) I see.

Queenie: You want my mother?

Sedgwick: Yes. Is she in?

Queenie: No, but she will be in any time.

Sedgwick: Can I wait? I'd like to see her.

Queenie: Yeh: that's okay. Make yourself at home, eh. Just a
                tick.

                *She carries the gramophone and records inside. Sedgwick
                looks around, with interest. Queenie returns.*

Queenie: You the new Minister?

Sedgwick: Yes.

Queenie: What's your name?

Sedgwick: Athol Sedgwick. I know yours: Queenie Mataira.

Queenie: Got it on your books, I suppose . . . Is it dull, being a
                Minister?

Sedgwick: No, never.

Queenie: Is it hard, doing good?

Sedgwick: Sometimes. It's harder, being good.

Queenie: (*curiously*) Were you in the war?

Sedgwick: Yes. Bomber pilot.

Queenie: Golly! You big brave fellow, eh.

Sedgwick: No.

Queenie: Kill anyone?

Sedgwick: Thousands, probably.

Queenie: Get any medals?

Sedgwick: Yes, two.

Queenie: Why don't you wear them?

Sedgwick: I gave them back, Queenie.

Queenie: Why?

Sedgwick: You see, I was so high up, I couldn't see what I was doing. I thought about it later. Then I could see.

Queenie: (*shrewdly*) Do good now to make up for the bad, eh?

Sedgwick: (*astonished at her insight*) Quite right.

Queenie: Mmm. You know: my Dad was a preacher. Full of the Gospel.

Sedgwick: (*interested*) Was he?

Queenie: Oh, he didn't wear a collar. Just walked about, telling everyone about God. Ma wants Johnny to be a preacher. That's my brother.

Sedgwick: Really?

Queenie: (*flatly*) Yeh. Spread the Word of the Lord . . . Do you like your collar back to front?

Sedgwick: I'm used to it now.

Queenie: Does it tickle?

Sedgwick: (*laughing*) No.

Queenie: Listen: you going to marry off Sylvia Atkinson?

Sedgwick: Yes, tomorrow afternoon.

Queenie: Know all your words?

Sedgwick: Well, I have my book, so if I forget, I can read them, Queenie.

Queenie: Do you like my dress?

Sedgwick: Mmm. Pretty.

Queenie: Then you'll see it tomorrow. It's all I've got for the wedding.

Sedgwick: Then you'll look very nice.

Queenie: I hate it. It's old. I love pretty things and dressing up. Like marriage.

Sedgwick: Is that what marriage is?

Queenie: You bet: all in white, everyone looking at me, a crown on my head . . .

Sedgwick: A crown?

Queenie: Don't you think a girl called Queenie should wear a crown?

Sedgwick: Yes. I suppose she should.

Queenie: Queenie's not my real name. It's Isobel. After Mrs Atkinson. I called myself Queenie when I was little. I always wanted a crown . . . You from the Old Country, aren't you?

Sedgwick: Yes, I am.

Queenie: Tell by your voice. Seen the Queen?

Sedgwick: Yes, I did once.

Queenie: Did she wear a crown?

Sedgwick: Not when I saw her.

               She has been circling round him, firing her questions and

Sedgwick finds her delightful.

You work for Mr Atkinson, don't you, Queenie?

Queenie: Yes, like Ma and Johnny. Only till next year, though. Then I go nursing.

Sedgwick: Will you like that?

Queenie: I suppose so. Bit scared of sick people. Keep me out of mischief, Ma says.

Sedgwick: You're the only Māori family left here now, I believe.

Queenie: Oh, yeh. Long time ago now. Tribe's all gone, to Tamatea. That's on the East Coast. You know, we used to own all of Te Parenga? Then we sold the land, bit by bit, till there was only this little piece left. All had to go. Nothing to do here. Last one to leave was my Uncle Joe. See this tree? (*Giggling, she goes to the pōhutukawa.*) Said he wouldn't go, so he climbed up with a dozen bottles of beer. Said they'd have to pull him down. Didn't need to: he drank all the beer and fell down.

Sedgwick: (*smiling*) Do you miss your own people?

Queenie: Oh, I never knew them, really. Seem to have lots of fun down there. Always asking us to come and see them. But Ma won't let us go.

Sedgwick: I see.

Queenie: You're better looking than the last one.

Sedgwick: Whoa there, Queenie; you'll turn my head.

Queenie: Do all the ladies fall for you?

Sedgwick: Look, Queenie: isn't there something you should be doing for your mother?

Queenie: Done it. Nothing now till she comes . . . Do I worry you?

Sedgwick laughs and sees over her shoulder, Aroha Mataira. She is a noble-looking woman of sixty, with the features of the aristocratic strain, somewhat beaked and aquiline. It is a face in repose of epic grief, in animation of wonderful warmth. Her dress is long and dark and she wears a wide-brimmed straw hat. She carries a flax basket.

Aroha: It must be Mr Sedgwick. I did not know that you would be calling.

Sedgwick: (*shaking hands*) How do you do, Mrs Mataira. Mr Carrington told me much about you. A power in the Church, he said. Put all the Pākehās to shame.

Aroha: Did he? That was too kind of him. I shall miss Mr Carrington. How he roared in the pulpit. Do you roar too?

Sedgwick: I need much more practice.

Queenie: Ma: isn't he good-looking! Much better than Mr Carrington.

Aroha: Hold your tongue. One does not say such things to a Minister. Are the pipis ready?

Queenie: (*sulkily*) Yeh.

Aroha: Here are corn cobs and tomatoes. And some pūhā from the orchard. Go inside and get them ready.

She gives the basket to Queenie who takes it inside with a bad grace. There is a cane chair on the porch: Aroha moves towards it, but Sedgwick reaches it first.

Aroha: Thank you. Over there. We can take the breeze with our talk. Queenie: bring another chair!

Sedgwick places the chair in front of the porch. Queenie appears with another battered cane chair, plumps it down and disappears.

(*Sitting*) Sit down, Mr Sedgwick.

Sedgwick: (*sitting*) Mrs Mataira: I ought to tell you that this is not merely a social call.

She looks at him enquiringly.

I have received a letter.

Aroha: A letter? What letter?

Sedgwick: (*drawing one from his pocket*) It came addressed simply: 'The New Minister, Parenga.'

Aroha: (*suddenly rigid*) What is the postmark?

Sedgwick: (*peering*) Tamatea.

Aroha: (*softly*) They lost no time . . . What does it say?

Sedgwick: (*handing it to her*) Read it.

Aroha: I need my glasses. Please read it to me.

Sedgwick opens the letter and hesitates.

What is it, Mr Sedgwick?

Sedgwick: There are things in it . . .

Aroha: (*grimly*) I can guess them. Read them all.

Sedgwick: (*reading*) 'To the New Minister at Te Parenga. Man of God, greetings from the . . . Garty er . . .'

Aroha: Ngāti-Raukura. The name of my tribe.

Sedgwick: 'Te Parenga, where you now preach the Word of God is the ancestral home of the . . . Ngāti-Raukura . . .?'

She nods.

'Our Kinswoman, Aroha Mataira, still lives there on land that belongs to us and her. She is a proud woman, tough and stubborn as an old stump. For ten years, we have been asking her to sell the land and come to us in Tamatea. But she likes better to grow old at Te Parenga, working like a slave for the Pākehā Atkinson, whose ancestors took our land from us. Her two children live there with her, in a world neither Māori nor Pākehā. Man of God: she will listen to you, but not to us. Use your power with

her to sell the land for the good of those who own
it with her. We need now money urgently to build a
hall where the young can dance and the old gather.
We ask you, Man of God, to entreat the Pākehā
Atkinson to add her land to his, for like all Pākehās
he has a greed for land. One bite more: he will be
happy. May Aroha Mataira then come to us with her
children where she can take her place as leader of the
Ngāti-Raukura. We would honour and cherish the
granddaughter of the great Whetumarama. Eagerly
will we await your reply, which will come like the
music of flutes to we who sign our names . . .' I'm
afraid I can't read the names.

A silence.

Aroha: (*broodingly*) Slice by slice from the whale.

Sedgwick: I beg your pardon?

Aroha: The great words of Whetumarama. My grandfather.
                To the British Governor.

Sedgwick: What were they?

Aroha: (*suddenly large and imposing*) 'God made this land for
                us. It cannot be sliced. If it were a whale, it could be
                sliced. Do you return to your own country which was
                made by God for you.'

Sedgwick: Magnificent.

Aroha: A dance hall! That the Ngāti-Raukura should come to
                this! Te Parenga's sacred ground for a dance hall!

Sedgwick: (*remembering Queenie*) Do not young people like to
                dance?

Aroha: Swilling beer and going to seed; a lot of laughing
                clowns for the Pākehā to gape at. Euh, I can see them.
                Once I went there, five years ago. I came back sick to
                my heart. My tribe had rotted, rotted away.

Sedgwick: Forgive me: I am a newcomer and don't yet know
your ways. But are you wise, Mrs Mataira, to cut
yourself away from your own people?

Aroha: (*rising*) Man of God: you are on the site of the greatest
victory ever won by the Māori over the Pākehā. Look
over there. What do you see? The oranges and lemons
of the Atkinson orchard. See instead a great tōtara
forest. And here, where my house stands. See the
pekerangi where the warriors crouched, muskets set
to fire. Down there on the beach, where those Pākehā
children play, see the great ship *Alcestis*, white sails
spreading, moving into Te Parenga Bay. Four hundred
soldiers aboard her, red coats and crossed straps.
And here, where this old pōhutukawa stands, see the
pūwhara of Whetumarama where he took his stand,
like a star shining in glory, his taiaha raised to strike.
Queenie! Queenie! Bring the taiaha of Whetumarama!

She begins to mutter to herself, an old battle chant.

> Ka whawhai, ka whawhai, e he!
> Ka whawhai, ka whawhai, e ha!
> Ka whawhai, ka whawhai, ki roto ki te awa . . .

*Queenie appears, bearing a ceremonial, carved spear,
which she gives to her mother and stands by the porch,
watching. Aroha moves up to the tree.*

Aroha: The Pākehā captain got as far as here: placed a
ladder against the pūriri wall and climbed half
way up. Face to face he came with Whetumarama:
Māori and Pākehā, holding each other's eyes. Then
Whetumarama raised his arm and sss! the taiaha sped
to the captain's heart. Down he fell, down, down,
bleeding his life into Te Parenga's earth. With that it
was all over. The Pākehā fled, leaving behind him two
hundred dead, lying out there like great patches of
blood. The great ship *Alcestis* spread its wings, borne
away on the great wave of fear. Te Parenga pā was

never taken by force. Only by time; Pākehā time. Slice
by slice from the whale: by time. You ask me to leave
this place, hallowed by blood. I will not. I stay here, in
the shadow of this old pōhutukawa. It was planted by
Whetumarama himself. On the day after the battle,
he planted it where the Pākehā captain fell, that its red
flowers might be a sign of blood between Māori and
Pākehā for ever. (*She shudders.*) Euh, how he hated
them! I too, hated them. Until He came to me.

Sedgwick: (*fascinated*) Who?

Aroha: The Lord Jesus.

Sedgwick is taken aback by the majesty of her statement.

(*With a painful intensity*) He came to me in a dream.
Glory was on His face. Abide, He said, abide. Keep
my covenant between Māori and Pākehā. Let my
Cross be your guide . . . It was late: I rose from my
bed and took this taiaha in my hand. I went to the
Church, your church. I had never been there before.
There He was, hanging like a fly by the nails, blood on
His hands, His feet, His poor, poor side. (*Her voice is
clogged with emotion.*) The moon shone on the stained
glass and played on His Head. I fell to my knees. I
took Him then as my King, the great Ariki of my
soul. And I gave Him this. I offered it to Him as the
sign of peace between Māori and Pākehā. It is holy,
blessed. And I stay in Te Parenga to keep my trust.
This last acre, this last slice from the whale, I keep
for Whetumarama and for his peace with Jesus the
Christ. No tree is cut, no stone disturbed. It is a holy
place, now and forever.

*She lightly touches the taiaha with her lips and gives it to
Queenie who receives it with awe and goes into the house.*

Sedgwick: You make me ashamed. Ashamed for my race.
Scouring the world for land and money. A trail of
blood everywhere.

Aroha: Your Christ came in that trail. He knows every shame, every dishonour. All the wounds of the world. And His love to heal them.

Sedgwick: Yes.

Aroha: Do you see then: I cannot betray Him for a dance hall.

Sedgwick: Yes, I see that. But your children: do they share these feelings?

Aroha: Āe. Because I keep alive in them the traditions of my race. Would they get that at Tamatea? Where the Gospel is derided? Where all that counts is pleasure and growing fat? Here we labour together. Mr Atkinson is a fine man; his people have been here three generations. Side by side we labour; together we heal the ravaged land of Te Parenga, make it fruitful. In a year my daughter will go nursing: heal the ravaged body. And soon will my son complete what his poor father could not: spread the Word of God to heal the ravaged soul.

               A pause.

Sedgwick: Has he a vocation for this?

Aroha: He will find it.

Sedgwick: How, Mrs Mataira?

Aroha: God will speak to him. As He does to my people when they work the fruitful earth.

Sedgwick: And then?

Aroha: I send him to you.

Sedgwick: To me?

Aroha: You are now the bearer of Christ in Te Parenga.

Sedgwick: Of course, if there is anything I can do—

Aroha: Mr Carrington told me to look upon him as the

father of my children when my husband died. I trust
you will do the same.

Sedgwick: I will. You may trust me. (*He rises.*) All right then, Mrs
Mataira. I know what to say to the Ngāti-Raukura.
You've made it very clear. And thank you—for a deep
experience.

Aroha: I like you. I feel a spirit in you. And a strength.

Sedgwick: Thank you. Well now, we'll soon meet again.

Aroha: We shall be at early communion on Sunday.

Sedgwick: But the wedding? Tomorrow?

Aroha: Ah yes, the wedding.

They are moving up towards the porch.

Sedgwick: Till tomorrow then.

*The sound of galloping hooves which approach and stop.
Then a long melodious call hangs on the air.*

Aroha: (*her face alight*) That's him.

*Johnny Mataira runs in. He is a fine-looking lad of
eighteen, wearing jeans and open shirt.*

Johnny: (*excited*) Ma!

Aroha: You were a long time, Johnny.

Johnny: I couldn't stop her! We did the beach four times! She
could be a racehorse: win everything!

Aroha: My son has been exercising Miss Atkinson's horse,
Jezebel. Johnny: Mr Sedgwick.

Johnny: (*shaking hands*) I am very glad to know Mr Sedgwick.

Sedgwick: I am glad to know you. Your mother has been telling
me about you.

Johnny: Has she? Bad or good?

Sedgwick: You'll pass.

Johnny: What do you think of Te Parenga, eh Minister? You going to like it here?

Sedgwick: I'm sure I am.

Johnny: And what do you think of the Māori, eh Minister?

Sedgwick: (*smiling*) Well, Johnny; from what I've heard, they go to Church every Sunday, they work hard, they're good to their mothers . . .

Johnny: You talking about us, eh. You like us: good. We have to do big things here. Be sure the Māori not forgotten in Te Parenga.

Sedgwick: (*with interest*) What do you want to do, Johnny?

Johnny: Something big! Something to leave a mark on the world! . . . Dunno what, yet.

Aroha: He's still a child for all he's a grown man.

Sedgwick: He's got time to grow up yet. Well, goodbye again. Is Queenie there?

Aroha: Queenie! Mr Sedgwick is going now.

Queenie comes out onto the porch and the family stands together, Aroha in the middle.

This is the Ngāti-Raukura, Mr Sedgwick. This branch won't be cut down.

Sedgwick: Goodbye.

He goes. Both children are a little uncomfortable. Queenie wriggles away and goes back into the house.

Johnny: He's a nice fellow, eh Ma?

Aroha: He'll be a good man. He'll help us.

Johnny: How, Ma?

Aroha: To reach God, boy.

Johnny sits down on the step.

Johnny: (*softly*) You know, Ma, I don't think we'll ever reach Him. He's so far away from here.

Aroha: No, boy. He's here. Right here with us.

Johnny: (*closing his eyes*) I can't see Him. I wish God was something you could see.

Aroha: Look inwards, boy. You'll see Him there.

A pause.

Queenie: (*from inside*) Come and get it!

Aroha: Come, boy.

Johnny: (*rising*) In a minute, Ma. First I have to rub Jezebel down. Put the cover on her.

Aroha: Yes, you must do that. Then ride her back, after. Don't be long now.

She looks at him, bends her head and brushes his forehead with her lips, goes in. Johnny stands a moment, then takes from inside his shirt a worn exercise book, covered with drawings. He turns over the pages, then moves stealthily along the porch. Keeping his eye on door and window, he lifts one of the boards stealthily and drops the book in. Then he looks down and draws out a gaudy comic and very furtively, a half-bottle of whisky and stares at it.

The sound of an approaching car.

Johnny, in a panic, replaces everything and runs off. The snort of a horse.

Voice: (*off*) Hello, Johnny. Come up, will you? We've something to tell you.

Mrs Atkinson and her daughter Sylvia enter. Sylvia carries a suitcase. Mrs Atkinson goes to the porch and knocks. Aroha appears.

Aroha: Mrs Atkinson! And Miss Sylvia! How do you do?

Sylvia: Hello, Mrs Mataira.

Aroha: Sit down a moment.

Mrs Atkinson: Oh, I can't stay. I've got Mr Atkinson in the car
and he hates to be kept waiting.

Sylvia: He couldn't be crabbier than he is now, Mother. After
a whole day in town.

Aroha: A moment you can, surely.

Mrs Atkinson: Five minutes then, no more.

Aroha: Good!

*Sylvia moves thankfully towards a chair but her mother
frowns at her. The two elder ladies sit. Queenie has
appeared at the window and is staring at Sylvia with
unabashed curiosity.*

Aroha: (*seeing her*) Queenie, bring out the tree tomato wine.
We must drink Miss Sylvia's health.

Mrs Atkinson: (*alarmed*) Please, Mrs Mataira. Don't go to any
trouble.

Aroha: A girl does not get married every day. A bride's health
must be drunk. It is the rule.

*Aroha turns to instruct Queenie. Mrs Atkinson and
Sylvia exchange resigned glances. Johnny appears, holding
a very grubby towel.*

Aroha: Queenie: you know where the wine is. Under the
sink. Johnny: bring three glasses.

Johnny: Only three?

Aroha: Three, I said.

Mrs Atkinson: Oh, I think this once you might break your rule.
I know you're very strict with them and quite right
too, but if it's the wine my husband put down last
summer, it wouldn't sozzle a fly, really.

Aroha: Three glasses. (*As Johnny goes, disgruntled*) See that they are clean! (*To Sylvia*) We are all so pleased that you will be married at Te Parenga.

Mrs Atkinson: Oh, don't give her the credit for that. If Sylvia had her way, she'd rush into a wayside chapel. Or even a registry office, I shouldn't wonder. No, I said. This is my show. You play your part and let me have my fun.

Sylvia: Yes, with that awful Claude Johnson making his frightful jokes and the place full of people I've known since I was so high, all giggling and staring—

Mrs Atkinson: What's the matter with you, Sylvia? That's what a wedding is! And you couldn't have a nicer place for it than Te Parenga. Could she, Mrs Mataira?

Aroha: No.

Mrs Atkinson: Come come, child: you were born here!

Sylvia: (*resigned*) I know, mother.

Johnny and Queenie appear with a bottle and glasses which they place in front of Aroha on a small wooden stool. Aroha rises to pour.

Johnny: Has he come yet, Miss Sylvia?

Sylvia: Who, Johnny?

Johnny: The man who's going to marry you.

Sylvia: (*drily*) Well, he's in the city, Johnny. I'm hoping to see him tomorrow.

The ladies now have their drinks.

Aroha: Miss Sylvia. To your happiness.

Sylvia: Thanks, Mrs Mataira.

Aroha: Te Parenga will miss you.

Johnny: What's his name, Miss Sylvia?

Sylvia: George Rawlings.

Johnny: And what is Mr Rawlings like?

Aroha: (*severely*) A foolish question. He is a very nice young man or Mrs Atkinson would not marry her daughter to him.

Mrs Atkinson: I'm afraid it wouldn't matter much whether I liked him or not. Sylvia would still go ahead. But I do like him. He's a very nice, solid young man.

Sylvia: He's not a weight-lifter, mother.

Mrs Atkinson: But he is solid, dear. You can't deny that.

Johnny: Does he like the Māori, Miss Sylvia?

Sylvia: I really couldn't say, Johnny. He has a number of them working for him. I guess they get along all right.

Queenie: Is the dress finished?

Sylvia: Yes, it's quite finished.

Queenie: Will you wear a crown?

Sylvia: No, just a veil.

Queenie: You excited?

Sylvia: Yes, I suppose I am, rather.

Queenie: You'll be the big thing of the whole show. Everybody staring at you. Just like you were the Queen.

Sylvia: I'll be glad when that part of it's over.

Mrs Atkinson: (*exasperated*) I'm surprised at you, Sylvia. The biggest moment of a girl's whole life. You just deck up, mother fusses round, father pays the bills and then you talk as if it's a bore for you.

Sylvia: You know I hate being on show.

Mrs Atkinson: No fun having daughters, is it Mrs Mataira?

Queenie: How many children you going to have?

Aroha: (*sharply*) Queenie.

Sylvia: (*frigidly*) I don't know, Queenie.

Queenie: (*dreamily*) I want six. Six of each kind.

Sylvia glances at her mother, gets an answering nod.

Sylvia: Johnny: how's Jezebel behaving? Has she taken to you?

Johnny: She hasn't thrown me yet, Miss Sylvia.

Sylvia: How would you like to keep her for a while?

Johnny: (*after an ecstatic pause*) Miss Sylvia! You mean that?

Mrs Atkinson: Sylvia won't need Jezebel until she's properly settled in at her farm at Hawke's Bay. But you'll have to look after her, Johnny. Feed her, groom her, ride her every day.

Johnny: I will do that, I will! Ma!

Aroha looks over to him, nods gently.

Mrs Atkinson: Good, then. That's settled. Suitcase, Sylvia.

Sylvia goes for the suitcase.

Mrs Mataira, what will you be wearing tomorrow? If you don't mind my asking?

Aroha: My blue silk and a new black hat.

Mrs Atkinson: (*receiving suitcase*) How nice . . . Well, I know this sounds awful cheek, but Sylvia's leaving a good many of her clothes here and she won't be needing them again. I could give them to the City Mission, but I thought Queenie might have some use for them. There are two dresses here and a hat.

Aroha: (*firmly*) Thank you for your kindness. Queenie does not need them, Mrs Atkinson.

Queenie: Oh, Ma! Let's see! Let's see them!

Mrs Atkinson: (*uneasily*) You wouldn't want to wear them out anywhere; they've had plenty of use . . .

Aroha: (*coldly*) Queenie has everything she needs, Mrs
                  Atkinson.

Queenie: (*imploring*) Ma, please! Just let's see them!

Mrs Atkinson: Don't be offended, Mrs Mataira. Please let her see
                   them.

> *A pause. Everyone looks at Aroha. Finally, she gives a stiff
> nod. Sylvia opens the case and holds up two simple print
> dresses. Queenie takes them, lovingly. Then she sees the
> hat, drops the dresses and jams the hat on askew.*

Queenie: Ma, look at me! Look at my hat!

Aroha: (*stiffly*) It is a nice hat.

Queenie: (*to Sylvia*) Tell Ma it suits me: quick!

Sylvia: Yes, in a way, it does. Goes with your skin.

Queenie: Ma, let me have it. Let me wear it to the wedding.

Mrs Atkinson: (*alarmed*) Are you sure you want to do that,
                   Queenie? That hat's rather well known at Te Parenga.

Queenie: I don't care. It's a hat. I've never had a real hat. Please,
                  Ma. Mrs Atkinson: help me.

Mrs Atkinson: I can't do that, Queenie. If your mother says so,
                   then it's all right. If she says no, then you can't. But . . .
                   I think she's weakening!

> *Aroha is not weakening at all.*

Aroha: (*suddenly savage*) Oh, keep the hat!

> *Queenie drops to her knees and embraces her mother.*

                  (*With contempt*) A foolish, vain, silly girl. What is a
                  hat? What can it do for you?

Queenie: (*imploringly*) It makes me look nice, Ma!

Aroha: Thank Mrs Atkinson.

Queenie: Gee, thanks, thanks Mrs Atkinson. (*She takes the hat* *off and turns it over, with great delight.)*

The toot of a car.

Mrs Atkinson: Oh, gracious, there's Mr Atkinson. Old fidget: he
gets so impatient. And there was just one other thing.
Can you come over early tomorrow, Mrs Mataira?
There's so much to do, you know . . .

Aroha: Of course. All of us?

Toot.

Mrs Atkinson: Oh dear. Yes, if you can. There's the marquee to
put up: Johnny, you can help there, big strong fellow
that you are; flowers to be cut—

Aroha: We shall be there at eight o'clock.

Mrs Atkinson: What would I do without you? Oh, and yes.
Afterwards, there'll be a lot of clearing up to do; we're
getting one young man in to help with the drinks—

Queenie, holding her hat, reacts; turns towards her.

—but we'll need you too. We'll pay you, of course . . .

Aroha: There is no need. If we can help, we are ready.

Mrs Atkinson: Lovely. Well now, that really is all. Goodbye, my
dear . . .

*Clive Atkinson appears, a bluff man of fifty, showing the
effect of years in the open air.*

Atkinson: What's keeping you girls! Talk, talk, talk. Oh, hello
Mrs Mataira. Queenie, Johnny.

Mrs Atkinson: All through Clive. Just coming.

Atkinson: Never knew two women like you, to take half an hour
when five minutes will do. Come along. I'm parched.

Mrs Atkinson: All right, dear. Goodbye, Mrs Mataira.

She moves off. Sylvia collects the suitcase and follows her.

Aroha: (*suddenly*) Could I speak to you, Mr Atkinson? Just for a moment?

Atkinson: Is it important?

Aroha: To me, yes.

Atkinson: (*after a moment's hesitation*) All right. You get down to the car, dear. Be down in a tick.

The ladies go.

Aroha: (*to Johnny and Queenie*) Take the glasses away. Or would you care for a drink?

Atkinson: (*observing what it is*) No thanks, Mrs Mataira.

Queenie and Johnny remove the glasses and table and go into the house.

Well?

Aroha: I have had Mr Sedgwick here. The Ngāti-Raukura have written to him from Tamatea. They want my land.

Atkinson: But they can't sell it without you.

Aroha: I know. But they talk of offering it to you. Asking you to buy it. Add it to your orchard.

Atkinson: Oh, I won't do that, Mrs Mataira. I've got quite enough to keep me busy. Of course, if ever I sold the orchard . . .

Aroha: (*alarmed*) Sell? Sell! But you love Te Parenga!

Atkinson: Of course I do. But land, you know: you can't just cherish it. There's more to it than that. Land pays or it's a burden. And if it's a burden, you sell it. And if things got bad and I had to sell, well, this land of yours would be very valuable to me. Access, drainage: couldn't be better.

Aroha: This land is sacred to my people.

Atkinson: Yes, Yes. I know how you feel. Well don't worry. I'm
                not likely to sell with prices the way they are. But—
                I've been meaning to say it—don't live in the past too
                much, will you now? Land must be used sometime,
                not just remembered. All things come to an end, you
                know.

                She turns away from him.

                Is that all?

Aroha: Yes.

                Rapid and impatient toots.

Atkinson: Now they're tooting me! Cheek of it. Tit for tat, I
                suppose. (*He moves off, a little disturbed by her, pauses
                by the tree.*) Nice old tree, this. Watch the roots,
                though. They're coming through here and there.
                Needs earthing up. See you tomorrow! (*He goes.*)

Aroha: (*faintly*) Goodnight.

                *Silence. Aroha stands by the tree. Queenie's voice is heard,
                singing 'Moonlight Becomes You' and Aroha turns away
                from this impatiently. The horse snorts off, then a long,
                high-pitched whinny. Aroha looks above her head at
                the tree. There comes a faint throbbing in the air, of a
                rhythmic and barbaric Māori chant. She walks to the
                end of the porch, staring out to sea. The chant swells,
                declines. Aroha turns back, passes through the door. The
                lights fade.*

Scene Two

*The wedding marquee, next day. It is of blue and white stripes, hung
on six-foot poles at the corners and at the centre by a pole making a
tall blue and white cone. Trestle tables and smaller tables for drinks.
The tent is crammed with guests, and heat is beginning to tell on them.
At the official table, the bride and groom, best man, bridesmaid,*

*bride's parents. Also sitting, Mr Sedgwick. Aroha cannot be seen.
When occasionally, the guests part to reveal her, she will be seen to be
wearing her blue silk suit and a large black hat of antic shape. Queenie
wears one of Sylvia's dresses and her hat. Johnny looks awkward and
uncomfortable in a thick blue suit. Roy McDowell in white shirt, black
trousers and bow tie, passes round drinks. George Rawlings is nearing
the end of his speech. There is a roar of laughter as the lights go up.*

George: (*with a rapid glance at his notes*) And so, on behalf of
my . . . wife!—

Laughter and cheers.

—and myself, I thank you for all the lovely presents
you have given us and for the good wishes that went
with them. If I may say so, it argues well—

Sylvia: (*hissing*) Augurs!

George: What? Oh. Augurs well for our future life together.

*He sits down. Loud applause. The guests break up, and
regroup. Dr Lomas, an old Scot and something of a card,
approaches the bridal table.*

Lomas: Listen everybody! I'm going to claim a very special
privilege! I'm going to be the first to kiss the bride.
And you know why? Because I was the first to see her.
Yes, at two o'clock in the morning, nearly twenty-one
years ago, I came to this house, did my stuff and there
she was, 7 pounds 12 ounces, a truly delectable little
morsel, squawking like a piglet.

Sylvia: Dr Lomas! You are awful!

Lomas: Never forget a birthweight. (*He looks round.*) Queenie?
Six pounds twelve. Johnny? Ay, a fine boy: eight
pounds two. (*He stares a moment at one of the guests.*)
No, Madam. You're not one of mine. Hawke's Bay, by
the look of you . . . So, because I'm the oldest friend
you've got, bar none! I'm claiming my rights. Stand up
girl. Give me your cheek, lass.

Sylvia stands, embarrassed. He kisses her. Cheers.

Right: first blood to me. Now it's open slather. Be in, lads.

Several rush to it, and Sylvia endures it with a good grace. The noise becomes hubbub. This is quelled by Claude Johnson, a cheer-leader born.

Johnson: Friends. Friends! Yes, there's going to be another speech. From me!

Groan.

Now, now, now. It won't take long. You all know me. I'm Claude Johnson, born and bred at Te Parenga. And it's my very pleasant duty to propose the health of Clive and Isobel Atkinson.

The guests prepare to drink, but he shouts them down.

Now I've known these young people a long time, longer than I care to tell you. Why, Clive and I were privates together; shared each other's sorrow and pain. And a lot more besides!

Laughter.

Clive: (*smiling, but urgent*) Sssh!

Johnson: Then Clive met Isobel, a whirlwind romance and Clive asked me to be his best man. So you see, I was in at the kill!

Mrs Atkinson: Oh really, Claude. Clive didn't bring down a dead duck!

Laughter.

Johnson: Isobel always pulled me up for my picturesquire speech, didn't you Iz? So you see, folks, I've known these people a long time and I'll tell you what they're made of. The best! Just the best there is.

Voices: Hear, hear.

Johnson: Now Clive's father, old Tom Atkinson, bought most of Te Parenga from an old Māori joker . . . What was his name, Clive? Whiti, Whoto . . .

Atkinson: Whetumarama.

Johnson: Yeh, that's it. Never could get my tongue round Māori.

The guests, as if by accident, clear to reveal the sombre face of Aroha.

The very land we're standing on was thick in virgin bush. It all had to be cleared by hand, cut down, burnt off. And when the land was clear it all had to be grassed: only tussock here, so the seed had to be brought from England, twelve thousand miles by sail: makes you think, doesn't it? And you know, in two generations, it looks like rolling English countryside. This fine old house: it'll last as long as an English castle and it's full of memories; built out of the best Te Parenga tōtara. It'll see all of us out, you bet. Well, Clive and Isobel stayed on at Te Parenga. Squire and squiress, they stayed on! I didn't, you know. Haven't lived here for thirty years. Nothing to keep me! I don't work the land: I only sell it. And every Christmas, I say to Clive: come on, you old sod, get out and see the world! What's this little one-horse joint forty miles from town, what's it got? Sell, boy, sell! Leave it to your Uncle Claude. He'll get you a good price for it!

Atkinson: And a good commission too, I'll bet.

Johnson: Well, I've got to live, Clive, same as you. But he won't. Just smiles and smiles and sticks on here like a limpet. And when I come back, well, you know: I can't blame him. The sun, the bare hills, old Rangitoto out there, the beach to walk on at night: makes me wish I'd never left it. So Clive stayed on and worked his land. Good on him. He's the salt of the Kiwi earth. So I ask you to charge your glasses and drink the health of Clive and Isobel.

All drink. Claude leads the guests, fortissimo and prestissimo in 'For they are jolly good fellows' and there are calls of 'Speech! Speech!' Clive Atkinson rises.

Atkinson: Mr Johnson: friends. You know, Claude's a trimmer. Trust him to try and make a sale in the middle of a wedding! Man: you're built on sand! Never mind: he's a good old stick and I'll give him his due. Thanks, Claude: thanks for everything. Well, friends: this is a sad day for us. No offence, George: you'll feel the same when your chicks leave the nest. There's only Mum and me now—

Mrs Atkinson: Don't call me Mum!

Atkinson: (*through laughter*) All right: Gran and me, sitting alone in our big house with no patter of tiny feet to liven it up . . .

George: Wait and see, Mr Atkinson!

Sylvia slaps his hand playfully.

Mrs Atkinson: (*through laughter*) Now don't think you can park your kids on me, Sylvia! I've done my dash!

More laughter.

Atkinson: But with the loss of our daughter, I'd like to say how pleased we are that a fine young man like George Rawlings is taking her away, and from what I can see, Sylvia, you couldn't be in better hands . . .

Guest: What about his arms!

Atkinson: Now, now. Don't embarrass the poor children. I suppose you know that George was by way of being an ace in the war. Flew hundreds of missions and got the DFC for bravery . . .

Sylvia: And bar, Daddy!

Atkinson: What? Oh, yes. And bar. Well, I'm proud of that. And I'm proud of this country. You know what all the boys said when they came back from the war: other places have their points, but there's no place anywhere like this. George did his job and what was that job? To keep this wonderful country for us. And when I think we've been here only a little over a century and we've fought in three wars . . . well, it makes me proud to be a Kiwi. So I'm going to give you a different toast, one you don't often hear at weddings but one I'd like to hear more often. I give you God's Own Country: New Zealand.

He is moved and his voice is husky. The guests murmur 'New Zealand' but drink self-consciously. One lady who has been waiting for just this opportunity, springs forward and like a choir-mistress, leads the assembly in 'God Defend New Zealand'.

Woman: (*piercingly*) 'God of Nations, at Thy feet . . .'

Everyone joins in the first line but no one knows any more and the New Zealand National Song peters out.

Woman: (*baffled*) Don't you people know our national song? Oooh! (*She retires, disgusted.*)

Guest: Hey! When are you going to cut the cake?

Sylvia looks at George and they rise uncertainly to perform their ritual. Mrs Atkinson, tearful, joins them. The knife is put in.

Johnson: (*irrepressible*) Come on, now, what about a song? What about the gayest little song to greet the happy pair? Sing, sing, sing! 'Why were they born so beautiful . . .'

All: 'Why were they born at all!'

Johnson grabs a large lady and brings her forward.

Johnson: This is my wife!

All: Hurray!

Johnson: And she's said she'll sing!

All: Hurray!

Mrs Johnson: (*furious*) Claude! I did not!

Johnson: Now then, Bertha, no pikers.

Mrs Johnson: (*weakening*) I don't know how I'll sing without a
                   piano.

Johnson: Give it a burl, old girl.

Mrs Johnson: I'll hit you in a minute. All right: I'll sing 'O
                   Promise Me', for Sylvia and George.

> *She stands by the bridal table, presses her hands together
> and sings. A rival group at the same time begins to sing
> quietly, 'You are my sunshine, my only sunshine' and this
> wins the contest. 'O Promise Me' is extinguished. Some
> of the guests form a kind of scrum, whirling round in a
> circle. The noise is raucous.*

Mrs Atkinson: (*rising*) Where are our Māoris? We want our lovely
                   Māoris! Mrs Mataira! Queenie! Johnny!

> *Johnny is discovered in the middle of the scrum, and is
> pushed forward, giggling. He is hazy with drink.*

Guest 1:   Come on, Johnny. Give us a haka, Johnny.

Johnny: Aw, no. Don't feel like it, eh.

Guest 2:   Yes! Ka mate, ka mate! Take it away, boy!

> *Johnny giggles foolishly.*

Guest 3:   Then give us a song! Waiata poi!

Queenie: I'll sing for you!

Guests: Hurray!

> *Queenie, perfectly self-possessed, begins 'I can't give you
> anything but love, baby' with astonishingly accurate
> command of rhythm and gesture. She has barely got out
> two lines of it when Aroha steps forward, her eyes flashing.*

Aroha: Stop that trash!

Tense, embarrassed silence. Queenie retires disgruntled.

I will sing.

Aroha bows to the bridal couple and begins. She has a voice of piercing sweetness, moving through the most delicate intervals, archaic, splendid. The song ends. Silence, then strong respectful applause. A buzz of conversation.

(*To Sylvia and George*) For you.

Sylvia: What was it, Mrs Mataira?

Aroha: An old love song of my race. And hopes for you to be happy together.

Sylvia: Thank you so much. George: wasn't it pretty?

George: Very. What do the words mean?

Aroha: Mr Rawlings: If I were to tell you, you would be shocked.

Some of the guests giggle.

I first heard it as a child, at Māori weddings. It is very sincere, very true, but in English: just as well to lock it away in my own tongue.

Atkinson: (*hurriedly, rising*) Thanks, Mrs Mataira. That was lovely . . . Well, friends, it's getting pretty hot in here. I suggest we adjourn to the garden or the house. My house is yours for as long as you want.

Guests: Hurray!

Sylvia and George rise and pass slowly out of the tent, followed by Mr and Mrs Atkinson and all the other guests. Only Aroha, Queenie and Johnny are left. Johnny is very drunk. His mother stands looking at him. He cannot meet her eye. He sits down heavily in a chair.

Aroha: (*severely*) You've drunk too much.

Johnny: (*laughing*) Yeh.

Aroha: I said to have one drink, Johnny. Only one.

Johnny: (*happily*) I know, Ma.

Aroha: You'd better go home and sleep it off. Queenie and I can manage.

Johnny: (*rising unsteadily*) Ma! I can fly! Watch! Watch me leave the ground! (*He whirls around and collapses.*)

Aroha: (*distressed*) Johnny! Wake up, Johnny!

Johnny, with every sign of happiness, starts to sing 'You are my sunshine'. He rolls over and stares up at his mother with every sign of bliss. Queenie giggles and helps herself to a cream-cake. Aroha glares at her. Atkinson comes in, weaving a little himself.

Atkinson: I thought there was a mad bull in here. Johnny! What's the matter?

Aroha: (*with dignity*) Johnny does not feel very well, Mr Atkinson.

Atkinson: One over the eight, eh? Well, it happens to all of us. Take him upstairs, Mrs Mataira. Let him lie down and cool off.

Aroha: He has disobeyed me. I said only one.

Atkinson: All mothers say only one. Now, Mrs Mataira: I couldn't let him drink lemonade at my daughter's wedding.

Aroha: You are a good man.

Atkinson: Nonsense: I just got a good memory. Come on: you take this side and I'll take the other.

Together, they get him to his feet.

Aroha: Queenie: you start packing up. I shall be back soon to help you.

Johnny: (*bawling*) 'You are my sunshine!'

Atkinson: (*indulgently*) Here. Quieten down.

Aroha: (*as they go*) I'm so ashamed.

Queenie alone. She giggles, then moves to the table and begins stacking food and glasses. Weary, she pushes her hat off her face. Hubbub outside. The bride and groom have appeared, ready to depart. The air is thick with ritual jocularity. When this is at its height, Roy comes in with an empty tray. He comes up to her silently, touches her arm. She stiffens but does not turn. Slowly, she turns her head and looks up into his face. He gives her a note. She opens it, reads it, looks scared, looks up at him again and finally, nods slowly. Roy presses her shoulder and moves away as Aroha comes in. Roy collects some bottles and moves out.

Aroha: Queenie: the young people are just off. Go and give your aroha to Miss Sylvia.

Queenie: (*dreamily*) Okay, Ma.

Aroha: Don't say okay!

Queenie moves out of the tent. Great hilarity.

Queenie: (*calling through the hubbub*) Goodbye, Miss Sylvia!

She returns. A car starts. Renewed cheers and shouting. Aroha, looking towards the departing pair, softly intones the close of her song. Queenie turns slowly towards her and their eyes meet. Then she turns away, preoccupied with her own thoughts. The lights fade.

Act Two

Scene One

Three months later, about six o'clock in the evening.

The interior of the Mataira house. Their living room is sparsely furnished: old carpet, battered sofa, table and two chairs. Door centre and the pōhutukawa hanging over it. The flowers have gone and it hangs somewhat lower over the porch. A fireplace and above it, two pictures: Holman Hunt's 'The Light of the World' and a heavily framed photograph of a tattooed Māori chief, Whetumarama. Leaning against the mantelpiece, the ceremonial taiaha. A door leads to the rest of the house.

Johnny is at home alone, dressed in his old orchard clothes, an open Bible on the table in front of him. He is paying no attention to it but drawing in his exercise book with fierce concentration. He holds the book up appraisingly and clicks his tongue.

Then he rises and tiptoes to the porch, making sure that no one is about. He kneels outside to remove his secret board and brings out a hat with a green feather in it and puts it on. Turns towards the bush and calls 'Jezebel!' An answering whinny. He dips into his treasure again, brings out a bottle of whisky, looks at it a moment, takes a deep swig. Gasps, says 'Boy, oh boy'. Then replaces the bottle and the floorboard, returns.

He bends over his drawing, putting finishing touches to it. He becomes aware of his breath, breathes urgently into cupped hands. Feels in his pockets, brings out a packet of chewing gum, extracts a pellet, chews industriously. Tests his breath again, is satisfied.

*He goes to the fireplace and takes the taiaha, puts it between his legs
and gallops round the room in elaborate pantomime, calls out 'Whoa,
Jezebel, whoa!' He confronts an imaginary adversary and his face
assumes a stylised expression of hatred.*

Johnny: Good morrow, Sheriff. At your dinner? Robbery pays,
I see . . . Yes, Robin Hood's the name. Why am I here?
Because I hate usurpers! You have taken our good
green land and you have despoiled our women! Have
at thee! Get back to France where you belong!

*The taiaha becomes a weapon of war. He uses it, lunging
and parrying, ducking and feinting, punctuating his
efforts with gasps of 'Aaah! Crrunch! Eek! Zowie!' etc.*

*Aroha appears on the porch, carrying a basket of
grapefruit. She looks through the window at him in
alarm, then throws open the door. A moment of taut
silence.*

Aroha: What are you doing? (*She sees the taiaha, takes it from
him.*) Don't ever touch that! You know: I don't have to
tell you! (*She puts it back against the wall.*)

Johnny: (*sheepishly*) Thought you wouldn't be back till late.
Thought you had to decorate the Church.

Aroha: The Church is finished. Mrs Atkinson helped me.
Take that silly hat off!

He removes it and throws it on the sofa.

Aroha: What are you chewing?

Johnny: Gum.

Aroha: Spit it out.

Johnny puts it behind his ear.

Throw it away.

Johnny moves towards the fireplace.

Outside!

Furious, he throws it outside. Aroha picks up the exercise book. He rushes to prevent her.

What is this?

Johnny:	Drawings.
Aroha:	I said to read the Book until I come back! . . . Robin Hood! Sheriff! Maid Marian! . . . Boy! Boy! When are you going to put away childish things and be a man!
Johnny:	(*sulkily*) Lots of people read about him. Men, too! You can see him on the pictures.
Aroha:	It is an old story. Nothing to do with life now. You can't live on stories.
Johnny:	The Book is full of stories.
Aroha:	That is different and you know why. The Bible is full of truth.
Johnny:	Robin Hood was true! He protected his land against invaders. And he was always kind to women. What is wrong with that?
Aroha:	Nothing is wrong with it. It has no meaning for us, that is all. (*She throws the book in the fireplace.*) Trash. I will not have trash in this house.

Johnny clenches his fists. Aroha sits down to unlace her shoes.

Where is Queenie?

Johnny:	You know she has gone to see Dr Lomas.
Aroha:	Yes I had forgotten. He will do nothing for her. A few pills and sign a paper.
Johnny:	She's been very crabby. For days.
Aroha:	We will wait tea until she comes.

She goes into her room. Johnny moves furtively to the fireplace.

Aroha: (*off*) I have news for you, Johnny. Miss Sylvia has sent for her horse.

Johnny rears as if struck. Aroha comes in.

Johnny: When?

Aroha: A horse float will call at ten tomorrow. Mr Atkinson said to have the saddle clean and the horse well groomed.

Johnny sinks onto the sofa, tense to the limit of endurance.

What is it, boy?

Johnny: I don't want her to go, Ma.

Aroha: It had to come.

Johnny: (*half to himself, inward and passionate*) She knows me. She answers when I call. Never thrown me: full of spirit, too. Sometimes I ride along the beach in the dark with the wind in my face and the waves breaking and spray gets in my hair. I'm in a great forest where horns sound. I want to shout and sing! . . . I don't want her to go, Ma.

Aroha: All things come at last, Johnny.

Johnny: Why have some people so much? Miss Sylvia lives on a great farm. If she wanted twenty horses she could have them. But no. She must have Jezebel, too. They have taken our land from us, they make us work for them—

Aroha: Boy, what are you saying? I work for them because I want to. And they bought our land from us! It is a good life we lead here. Together, Māori and Pākehā, we make Te Parenga fruitful.

Johnny: (*fiercely*) And who takes the fruit!

Aroha: (*after a pause*) Johnny: what is troubling you?

Johnny: Ma. I love that horse.

Aroha: It is not yours to keep.

Johnny: (*in anguish*) Ma. I've got nothing. I am nothing.
                Nothing!

Aroha: A man's worth is not reckoned by the things he has
                but by the spirit in him. You know that: the Book tells
                you.

Johnny: (*raging*) I hate the Book!

                *Aroha looks at him closely, then moves to the sofa and
                sits.*

Aroha: Come here, Johnny.

                He takes one pace towards her, sullen and unwilling.

                Listen, boy. To live in this world, you've got to be
                strong. God has no use for weaklings, snivelling after
                every little thing that takes their fancy. Look at Him
                up there.

                *Johnny gives 'The Light of the World' one brief glance
                and returns to his black rage.*

                There He is: The Light of the World. That light can
                find its way into the darkest heart. Open your heart
                to Him, Johnny. Let His light in . . . I can find you
                a place in the Book to put you at peace again. I want
                you to read it to me. Get it, Johnny.

Johnny: I don't want to. I don't want peace.

Aroha: You think that because you feel wounded and envious.
                Come. Read it to me and your envy will go.

                *Finally, unwillingly, he brings her the Bible. She finds a
                marked passage for him and gently pulls him down to sit
                at her feet.*

Johnny: (*ungracious, mumbling*) 'Lay not up for yourselves
                treasures upon earth, where moth and rust doth

corrupt and where thieves break through and steal,
but lay up for yourselves treasures in Heaven . . . for
where your treasure is, there will your heart be also.'

*He looks up at her, conceding nothing, but struck by the
relevance of the passage to his own feelings. She lays her
hand on his shoulder.*

'The light of the body is the eye; if therefore, thine
eye be single, thy whole body shall be full of light.
But if thine eye be evil, thy whole body shall be full of
darkness . . .' What's it mean, if thine eye be single? I
have two eyes.

Aroha:　　It talks of the inner eye, boy. Your soul, looking out
on the world.

Johnny:　　'Take no thought for your life, what ye shall eat, what
ye shall drink, nor yet for your body, what ye shall put
on. Is not the life more than meat and the body more
than raiment . . .' We'd look pretty funny without
clothes, Ma.

She smiles.

'Therefore, take no thought for the morrow. Seek ye
first the Kingdom of God and His righteousness and
all these things shall be added unto you. Sufficient
unto the day is the evil thereof.' (*He closes the book. A
silence.*) It's hard. It's hard not to think of tomorrow.

Aroha:　　It's hard but it pays you in gold. It's an open door to
the love of God.

Johnny:　　(*ruefully*) He doesn't make it too easy, does He?

Aroha:　　No. It's not easy.

Johnny:　　(*slowly, not looking at her*) Ma. You're a good woman. I
love you, Ma.

She sits rigid with pleasure.

Aroha:　　(*softly*) You'll give Jezebel back then? In good grace?

Johnny: You'll see your face in her flanks.

Aroha: (*rising, a glad lightness in her voice*) Come, boy. Let's
                prepare the meal. Dr Lomas must be very busy.
                Queenie has had to wait. We'll keep hers.

                They pass out of the room. A pause, and Queenie appears
                on the porch. She moves up to the door and suddenly
                throws it open. She looks wild and distracted. She comes
                in, throws her hat down and sits heavily in a chair.

Aroha: (*off*) Johnny: get me the two best grapefruit you can
                find.

                Johnny comes in.

Johnny: Hi, Queenie. You all right? Ma! Queenie's back!

                He searches among the grapefruit. Aroha appears at the
                door.

Aroha: You were a long time, Queenie . . . What's the matter?

                Queenie puts her head in her hands.

                (*Going to her*) Queenie! Queenie, girl. Something's
                happened.

Queenie: (*piteously*) Ma!

Aroha: (*agitated*) Something happened with Dr Lomas. Yes?

                Queenie nods.

                Are you ill?

                Queenie shakes her head, stops, nods.

                What do you mean? Tell me, Queenie!

                Queenie is still silent. Aroha pulls her to her feet.

                Queenie: tell me!

                Queenie cannot say the words; tries but cannot. Aroha
                comprehends. A long pause. Aroha and Johnny stand
                rigid. Queenie slowly sits.

Aroha: Whose. Whose!

Queenie: Roy McDowell's.

Aroha: Who is he? Johnny: do you know him?

Johnny: Chap at the pub.

Aroha: Pākehā?

Johnny nods.

Go and get him. At once. And bring Mr Sedgwick, too. Straight away, now!

Johnny dives out.

When did this happen?

Queenie: Three months ago.

Aroha: Often?

Queenie: Yes.

Aroha: Where?

Queenie: Up there. In the bush.

Aroha: When?

Queenie: After you had gone to bed.

Aroha: Slut. Slut!

Queenie: (*angry*) Don't say things like that, Ma!

Aroha: My daughter. The great granddaughter of Whetumarama. Reared in Christ. Taught to respect her past and her race and the sacred ground of Ngāti-Raukura. And she uses it for that! . . . That!

Queenie: Yes, for that! For love!

Aroha: Love. Love!

Queenie: (*passionately*) You don't know what love is. All wrapped up in Whetumarama and Him up there. I'm sick of it, sick of it. Rammed down my throat every day. It doesn't mean a thing! And I'll do it again, Ma. I will, I will, I will!

Aroha slaps her savagely across the mouth. Queenie cries out.

Queenie: (*slowly*) Don't you hit me, Ma. I'm having a baby.

Aroha stares at her.

Aroha: How old is he?

Queenie: Twenty-one.

Aroha: A baby. Just a baby. And do you like him, this baby of yours?

Queenie: (*hurt*) I like him okay.

Aroha: 'I like him okay.' A love speech, eh Queenie? Yes, yes. You know what love is.

Queenie: I don't care what you think. It's my life.

Aroha: Not till you're twenty-one, my girl. You want to marry this boy?

Queenie: Course I do.

Aroha: I can stop you, Queenie.

Queenie: (*shrewdly*) You won't do that.

Aroha: Why won't I?

Queenie: What about the Atkinsons?

Aroha: Don't mention their name! You've brought shame on me and shame on them, who've been so good to you.

Queenie: Then I'd better get married; quick too, eh Ma?

Aroha: (*heavily*) Yes. Yes. Yes, you'll get married. Yes, you'll go away with him somewhere, far away from here. Forget everything I've taught you. And when your child's born, there'll be another and another and another. A dozen of them, all crying for food. And if your man goes on the way he's started with you, there'll be other women to take your place when you're fat and ugly. All your life, I've tried to bring you up straight and clean. Teach you honour, respect, pride. You're pretty: you could have had a fine husband when you moved out into the world. But you go and fall for the first no-good Pākehā that comes along. Weak. Weak. After all my teaching. All right: that's your life. Now go and enjoy it.

Queenie: (*with dignity*) Perhaps I will, Ma. Perhaps I won't worry all the time what the Pākehā thinks of me. Perhaps I won't look ahead all the time, like you do. And perhaps, if I'm happy today, I won't be thinking about what tomorrow will bring. And then perhaps, tomorrow won't be so bad.

A pause.

Aroha: Queenie, Queenie! Why did you do it?

Queenie: Because I wanted to. That's why.

Aroha: Couldn't you have come to me?

Queenie: (*scornful, yet pitying*) Ma. Oh, Ma! . . . When will I get married?

Aroha: (*grimly*) Tomorrow, my girl. Tomorrow.

Queenie: But what about my dress?

Aroha: What dress?

Queenie: My wedding dress, Ma!

Aroha: What!

Queenie: I want to be all in white, a crown on my head.

Aroha: Queenie girl: have you gone out of your senses? Mr Sedgwick can't marry you in white.

Queenie: But why?

Aroha: A bride is untouched. You are not.

Queenie: I'll ask Mr Sedgwick.

Aroha: He'll say no.

Queenie: I'll ask him.

Aroha: (*shouting*) Ask then! But I know his answer.

She looks at Queenie and her face twitches. She turns away to hide a smile, sits down on the sofa, suddenly quite calm.

Queenie: (*coming up to her*) Can't I have just a little orange blossom in my hair? Make me smell nice?

Aroha laughs suddenly.

Aroha: Vanity, vanity, all is vanity. All right. Ask the Minister. See what he says.

Queenie sits on the floor beside Aroha.

Queenie: I think you'll like Roy, Ma.

Aroha: He'd better be nice.

Queenie: He loves me a lot. Said so, dozens of times.

Aroha: That's something, then.

Queenie: You've seen him, Ma. At the wedding.

Aroha: (*unfavourably impressed*) That boy!

Queenie: Oh, I know he looks a bit tough. But he's not like that really. I know, you see.

Aroha: (*turning to look at her*) You wicked girl.

Queenie: Yes, I am. I'm wicked. But I like it, Ma.

Aroha: (*gently*) Hold your tongue.

The sound of the men approaching. Johnny arrives with Sedgwick and Roy. Johnny stands aside for Sedgwick to enter. Roy stands outside in an extremity of embarrassment.

Sedgwick: (*beckoning him in*) This is Roy McDowell, Mrs Mataira.

Aroha looks at him carefully.

Well, it looks as if I have the floor. Queenie is expecting a child and Roy admits to being the father. Right?

Roy: Yeh. So far.

Sedgwick: Well, these things have happened before and no doubt they'll happen again. With a little understanding we can sort it all out. Now: answer me honestly. Has this sort of thing happened to you before?

Roy: Not this way, it hasn't.

Sedgwick: All right, then. Well, obviously the first thing for you to do is get married as soon as possible. I can get a special licence and marry you the day after tomorrow. How's that?

Queenie: Mr Sedgwick?

Sedgwick: Yes, Queenie?

Queenie: Can I wear a white dress? With a veil and a crown?

Sedgwick: You mean: dress as a bride?

Queenie: Yes. With orange blossom.

Sedgwick: No, Queenie. I'm afraid you can't. Not in my Church. A rule's a rule, and I'm going to stick to it.

Queenie: Oh, don't give me that. It's only a show, the Church stuff. If I'm going to be married, I want my show too. I want lots of people and everybody looking at me, saying, see that girl up there: that's Queenie Mataira, isn't she lovely. You'll hear 'Here comes the Bride', and I'll be on Mr Atkinson's arm; he always said he'd give me away . . .

Sedgwick: I'm afraid Mr Atkinson might feel a little differently . . .

Aroha: None of this must even get to Mr Atkinson! He won't give you away: how could he?

Queenie: What's it to him? I'm getting married, aren't I? I'm still me, aren't I? What's changed about that?

Aroha: (*fiercely*) There will be no guests, understand? No guests, no music, no Atkinsons, no party. And you will go away as soon as it is over.

Queenie: Where to?

Aroha: That's for your husband to say.

All look at Roy.

Roy: There's just one thing you're all forgetting. Me.

Sedgwick: What do you mean?

Roy: (*acting tough*) It's pretty clear what I mean, isn't it?

Aroha: You got my daughter into trouble. You marry her now and give her your name.

Sedgwick: It's the honourable thing to do.

Roy: Yeh? Well, maybe I'm not so honourable . . . You've all taken it for granted. Well, I'd just like to let you know that it's not cut and dried, that's all. I don't have to marry Queenie. There's no law says I have to.

Queenie: (*appealingly*) But you will, Roy, won't you? You will, won't you?

Roy: (*gently*) I can't, Queenie.

Queenie: Roy!

Aroha: Why?

Roy: I just can't, that's all.

Sedgwick: You'll have to make some explanation, young man. You can't just leave it at that.

Roy: You can't force me to marry and you can't force me to talk about it.

Queenie: Don't you love me, Roy? That what it is?

Roy: (*troubled*) You know I'm fond of you, Queenie. More
                than any . . . You know that.

Queenie: Then what is it? Roy: tell me.

Roy: (*lamely*) You're too young. You're only seventeen.

Aroha: She has my consent. I don't want to give it, but I give
                it.

                Silence.

Sedgwick: Look, young man. I know you don't go to Church
                or abide by its commandments. I know what you
                think of parsons. Kill-joys, aren't we? Always stopping
                people having fun. Well, you've got to pay for fun.
                And that's where we Bible-banging drearies come
                in. To show you where fun ends and responsibility
                begins. And it's my job to show you where your duty
                lies—

Roy: Aw, don't give me that—

Sedgwick: Don't interrupt me, please! It's quite clear what you
                must do. This girl will bear your child and you must
                acknowledge it by marriage. That's all there is to it.

Roy: (*slowly*) That's all there is to it. All right you've asked
                for it. Queenie's a Māori, don't you understand?

Sedgwick: I know she's a Māori. Well?

Roy: How can I take her home with me? What will my
                folks say?

Sedgwick: You should have thought of that before.

Roy: It'd be a mixed marriage. Brown kids! I couldn't have
                brown kids!

Sedgwick: You'll be the father of one. And anyway, I'm told this
                country's full of mixed marriages. Good ones, too.

Roy: (*urgently*) Aw, but you don't know my folks. My
                Dad'd have a fit! And Mum: you don't know Mum.

I just don't know what she'd say: she hates anything like this! She wouldn't have Queenie in the house. I know she wouldn't! Her friends'd cut her dead! And I'm young: I've got my life before me! You've got to think of that! . . . I like the Māoris, always have, don't believe in colour bar, but . . . well, marriage is different, that's all . . . It shouldn't have happened! It shouldn't have happened!

Sedgwick: No, you're quite right: it shouldn't. But it's too late now.

Roy: I can't, I can't, I can't! It wouldn't be fair on Queenie!

Aroha rises with majestic calm.

Aroha: What are your parents?

Roy: My Dad's a grocer.

Aroha: A grocer. Is that so high and mighty, then?

Roy: No. They're good folks. Nothing special, I suppose, but they're my folks.

Aroha: Do you know that Queenie comes from a long line of chiefs? That she can trace her ancestors through twenty-five generations of Ngāti-Raukura?

Roy: Yeh. She told me.

Aroha: Is that not good enough for your mother?

Roy: Aw, what does it matter to my Mum that Queenie comes from a long line of chiefs? She'd just be a Māori to her. Look, Mrs Mataira. You can't live on that stuff now. Okay before the white man came, but now: well, this is a white man's country now.

A long pause. Aroha turns away slowly. From this point, she begins to crack.

Sedgwick: Well, that's your decision, is it?

Roy: (*in genuine distress*) Look, I'd like to. Honest I would. But I can't!

Sedgwick: Well, you know the law. It can't compel you to marry the girl; it can compel you to support the child if you admit paternity. You'll do that?

Roy: Yes, sure I will. I'll do my best for you, Queenie, honest I will.

She turns away from him and collapses at the table shaken by sobs.

God! Why does it have to be like this! The greatest thing in life and it has to end like this.

Sedgwick: If you'd listened to those who knew better, your good folks, as you call them, you'd have seen the way to deal with the greatest thing in life. All right: leave your address at my house. I'll see that the Court Order is prepared. You'd better go now. And take my advice: leave Te Parenga.

Roy: (*irresolute*) Yeh. I know I'm a bastard, but that's life, isn't it. Turns you into a bastard, whatever you do. Well, hooray Queenie. Thanks . . . for . . .

Johnny: (*roaring*) Get out! (*He seizes the taiaha.*) Get out, Pākehā, or I'll knock your head in!

Roy: (*with a feeble attempt at bravado*) Here, what's up? Okay, okay, I'll go.

He gives a quick, shamefaced look at them all, and leaves.

Johnny stands by the door a moment, taiaha upraised.

Aroha: (*gently*) Put it down, Johnny.

He lowers the spear and turns slowly to face her.

Sedgwick: Well, what's to be done, Mrs Mataira?

Aroha: She can't stay here. That's sure.

Sedgwick: I can get her into a home somewhere. She'll have to work for a few months and then the child can be adopted—

Aroha: No. She goes to Ngāti-Raukura, at Tamatea. They will have her, ask no questions, look after the child. She is one of them, now. (*To Queenie*) You go tomorrow. After your child is born, you are on your own, understand? Find yourself a job, a husband: what you like. I have finished with you.

Sedgwick: Come, come, Mrs Mataira. You can't mean that. She's been abandoned once. Don't you leave her too.

Aroha: What am I to her? What have I ever been? A mother who loves her? No. A gaoler. That's all: a gaoler. Well, she got out of gaol late at night. Look what happened. All right: let her try freedom. See if she does any better with that.

Queenie: (*defiantly, her grief forgotten*) Don't worry. I shall be okay.

Aroha: (*savagely*) You know what you've done! You've ruined our name! How can I work for the Atkinsons now? What will they think of me?

Sedgwick: But surely Mrs Mataira, there is no need for the Atkinsons to know why Queenie is going?

Aroha: Would you have me deceive them? I am a woman of honour, Mr Sedgwick. I shall tell them everything.

Sedgwick I think you're taking this far too seriously. I understand that it's really no disgrace . . . er . . .

Aroha: (*fiercely*) For Māoris, you mean? You've heard? This happens all the time to them? Can you not understand that honour and virtue are sacred things to me? Is that just for the Pākehā?

Sedgwick: Of course not.

Aroha: I made my rules. I lived by my rules. Queenie knew those rules. She breaks them: she goes!

Sedgwick: I would ask you to pray before taking this step. God will advise you if you listen for His voice.

Aroha: God knows I have tried to do His will.

Sedgwick: Are you sure it was His will? You must ask yourself that. Leave it to Him for a while. You will find that everything will blow over.

A pause.

Aroha: My world is blowing over.

Sedgwick: Come, that's not true. This is a dark tunnel for you. But there's always some light there, however dark it seems. Push on: find the light. Don't decide anything now. If you want my help for Queenie, it's there for you to use. Don't lose heart. And keep your chins up, all of you. (*He goes.*)

Silence.

Johnny: (*looking at the taiaha*) Keep your chins up. All the better for the Pākehā to kick at.

Queenie: Ma?

Aroha: Well?

Queenie: I'm hungry, Ma.

Aroha: (*wearily*) Yes. Yes, you must eat. Come. Help me prepare it.

Queenie rises and faces her. They hold each other's eyes a moment. Then Queenie moves slowly through the door. Aroha follows.

Johnny stands a moment, still, then puts down the spear and picks up the Robin Hood hat from the sofa, looks at it, and hurls it away from him. Picks up the spear again, goes onto the porch, lifts his floorboard and draws forth a bottle of whisky. A whinny, off. A sudden resolve grips him. Spear upraised, he runs out. Another whinny.

Aroha: (*off*) Johnny. Johnny!

She comes in, sees that the taiaha has gone. Alarm seizes her.

Johnny! Johnny!

Galloping hooves.

Johnny!

She rushes out of the house. The hoofbeats grow fainter, die. Aroha still calls his name.

Scene Two

Next morning.

Queenie sits, soberly dressed, a battered suitcase beside her. Atkinson's voice can be heard, off, calling 'Johnny! Johnny!' He arrives at the door and knocks, perfunctorily.

Atkinson: (*entering*) Hello, Queenie.

Queenie: Hello.

Atkinson: Where's your mother?

Queenie: Out.

Atkinson: Where's Johnny?

Queenie: Out too.

Atkinson: Where's my daughter's horse?

Queenie: Out with Johnny.

Atkinson: And why aren't you at work today? Where are you going?

Queenie: Away.

Atkinson: Where to?

Queenie: Tamatea.

Atkinson: Tamatea? To the Ngāti-Raukura?

Queenie: Yeh.

Atkinson: For a holiday?

Queenie: For good.

Atkinson: (*amazed*) What's happened to the Matairas this morning?

Queenie: We're in a mess, Mr Atkinson.

Atkinson: (*looking at her closely*) What kind of a mess?

Queenie: A proper mess.

Atkinson: (*after a pause*) Well, where's Johnny? Don't say 'out' again I can see that.

Queenie: (*flatly*) He went out last night on Jezebel, the taiaha in his hand. He didn't come back. Ma went out to look for him. She came back late: no sign of him. She went out again early this morning. That's all I know.

Atkinson: I suppose he knows a horse float will be here at ten.

Queenie: Must have forgotten.

Atkinson: A fine thing! What am I supposed to do?

Queenie: I don't know, Mr Atkinson.

Atkinson: And what about the orchard?

Queenie: You'll just have to find someone else, eh.

Atkinson: Yes, and you know how easy that is! (*Pause. He looks at her again.*) Are you in trouble, Queenie?

Queenie: Yes. Please don't ask me any more.

Atkinson: All right. You won't do anything silly, will you?

Queenie: Bit late now.

Atkinson: (*moving a step towards her*) Growing up, aren't you?

Queenie: Yes. Fast.

Atkinson: (*another step*) You're a pretty kid, too. Did you know that?

Queenie: (*staring at him steadily and coldly*) I thought you came here to see about your horse.

Atkinson: (*recalled to himself*) I did too, damn it! What's got into the boy: chasing girls?

Queenie: Don't ask me.

Atkinson: Always seemed so mature that boy. Horses, spears, galloping off into the night . . . Who does he think he is? Well, I suppose I'll just have to wait. Damned annoying. (*He goes to the door and stands looking out.*) Hello. Your tree's looking sick.

Queenie: Oh?

Atkinson: It's falling over. Tell your mother she'll need to get a strainer wire on it. Or cut it down.

Queenie: She'll never do that. She loves that tree.

Atkinson: Well, it's not much of a tree now. Break a window if it falls . . . Twenty past nine! I haven't got all day . . . Ah, here's someone! Looks like Sergeant Robinson! What's he want?

Sergeant Robinson strides onto the porch, the image of small-town authority.

Robinson: Ah, there you are, sir. Been chasing you since nine o'clock. Your wife said you were over here.

Atkinson: What is it, sergeant?

Robinson: Bit of bother, I'm afraid. Young Johnny Mataira. Can I come in?

Atkinson: Yes, come in.

Robinson enters.

Well? What's the boy done?

Robinson: Just done his best to wreck the Church, that's all.

Atkinson: What?

Robinson: Fact. Whole inside's a wreck. Prayer books all over the place, most of them torn out of their covers, all the altar gear smashed and every lead in the big window broken.

Atkinson: Good God.

Robinson: Place looks like a tornado's been through it.

Atkinson: But how did you—

Robinson: Heard it. Station's only two doors away. About two in the morning. First I heard a horse coming: that woke me up. Wondered whose it could be. Heard it stop. Then nothing for a while. Then all this banging and crashing. Rushed out and there he was, on top of the altar, sticking that spear of his through the window. Got there just too late. It's a write-off.

Atkinson: Oh now, this is serious. That window was given by my father. Cost a hundred and fifty quid in 1912; twice that now. By God, this is going to rock Te Parenga. Has he gone mad or something?

Robinson: That's just what it looked like. I tell you, when I came down the aisle and he turned and saw me, I swear for a moment he was going to put that damn spear right through me.

Atkinson: What did you do?

Robinson: Came up close, quietly, said: Hello, Johnny. That's a nice taiaha you've got there. I'd like to see it. He looked at me. All I could see were his eyes, glittering. Then I saw his fingers slowly unclench and he dropped it into my hand. Easy then. He started to cry! Never heard anything like it. Like a wolf, howling. Took him back to the station. Stayed the night.

Atkinson: Well, this beats all.

Queenie: What will you do with him?

Robinson: He'll come up on charge.

Queenie: What with?

Robinson: Wilful damage.

Queenie: Is that bad?

Robinson: Bad enough, in this case. Where's your mother?

Queenie: Out looking for him.

Robinson: Then I'll have to wait for her.

Atkinson: You are in a mess and no mistake, Queenie. Where's the boy now?

Robinson: Took the horse back to your place. Then straight back here.

Atkinson: Then he'll find me waiting for him.

Queenie: Will they put him in gaol?

Robinson: Don't know yet. Wait and see, eh.

Queenie: Oh, golly. Everything happening at once. Don't know what Ma will do.

Aroha appears, her face worn with strain. She starts with alarm when she sees Robinson.

Aroha: (*coming in rapidly*) Sergeant. Have you found my boy?

Robinson: (*soothingly*) Yes, Mrs Mataira. He's all right. Taken the horse over. Back any minute.

Aroha: Has he done wrong?

Robinson: He has.

Aroha: What was it?

Robinson: Wilful destruction.

Aroha: Where?

Robinson: In the Church.

                 Aroha sways slightly.

                 Now, then. Keep calm. He'll tell you the rest when he
                 comes.

Queenie: Ma. It's time for me to go.

Aroha: Yes. Would you gentlemen mind waiting outside a
                 moment? There is something I have to say to Queenie.

Robinson: Certainly, Mrs Mataira.

                 *The two men go outside but are visible on the porch. They
                 talk softly and occasionally glance indoors.*

Queenie: Shall I write to you? When it happens?

Aroha: Tell your Auntie Niania to let me know.

Queenie: Will I see you again, Ma?

Aroha: I don't know, Queenie. You know about your brother?

Queenie: Yes.

Aroha: (*urgently*) Swear you'll say nothing about it in Tamatea.

Queenie: All right, Ma.

Aroha: Go now, Queenie.

Queenie: (*crying*) Sorry, Ma. Kiss me?

                 *Aroha bends her head and touches Queenie's forehead
                 with her lips.*

                 Hooray, Ma.

Aroha: Goodbye, Queenie.

                 *Queenie picks up her suitcase and moves slowly past her.
                 Outside, she shakes hands with Atkinson and Robinson,
                 both of whom wish her luck. She looks back at her
                 mother through the window: no recognition. Queenie
                 shouts 'Hooray!' to the world, as it were, and trudges
                 off, indomitable.*

Come in now.

They come in.

What must I do, sergeant?

Robinson: Johnny will come up on charge next week, Mrs Mataira. He'll have to go down to Waikaru for the sitting. You must go surety for the sum of fifty pounds for your son's bail. You'll get it back, of course, after the case is heard. If you give it to me now, I'll fix it up with the Court.

Aroha: (*after a pause*) I shall get the money. (*She leaves the room.*)

Robinson: Poor, poor soul. Her world in pieces.

Atkinson: Well, what did you expect? I've seen this coming. Did you see Johnny at Sylvia's wedding? Out cold. Didn't occur to me at the time but now I see that it was the first crack. Queenie was the second. Quite typical. Wonder who it was.

Robinson: Well, don't look at me.

Atkinson: It's her, of course. All this Christian rubbish.

Robinson: (*uncomfortably*) That's a pretty strong thing to say, Mr Atkinson.

Atkinson: Well, I feel strongly. Christianity's all right for us. It's in our bones. We've had two thousand years of it. We know how far to take it and where to draw the line, but they don't. No judgement. No common sense. Swallow it all, hook, line and sinker. Get into a hell of a mess and start tearing the place apart.

Robinson: Oh now, wouldn't say that. Law and order: not so easy for them with their background. Not used to it. They see things a bit different. They'll come round to our way of thinking in time.

Atkinson: No sign of it yet. And they've had a hundred years.

Johnny appears on the porch holding the taiaha. He hears the rest of Atkinson's speech.

No. Scratch them, you'll find savages underneath, ready to break out into violence at the drop of a hat. They've begun to slip. And once they slip, they fall fast.

Johnny comes in quietly and puts the taiaha by the fireplace.

Johnny Mataira: there you are. I've just heard the whole extraordinary story. What on earth came over you?

Johnny: (*coldly*) I don't know, Mr Atkinson.

Atkinson: Do you know how much that window will cost to replace? And the other damage you've done? How do you think your mother's going to pay for it? Because I tell you one thing straight: I'm not going to.

Robinson: I think perhaps, Mr Atkinson, if you don't mind me saying it, they got enough to cope with just now—

Aroha enters with a worn roll of notes.

Aroha: Johnny.

Atkinson: Just tell me one thing. Johnny: had you been drinking?

Aroha: He never drinks, Mr Atkinson.

Atkinson: Wait a minute, now. I've seen him drunk, don't forget.

Aroha: Once, then.

A pause.

Johnny: Yes, I'd been drinking!

Aroha: Johnny!

Johnny: I bought a couple of bottles of whisky. Last week.

Atkinson: (*with a glance at Robinson*) How did you manage that, Johnny? You're under age.

Johnny: Chap at the pub. He got them for me. Who'll have a drink? (*He rushes outside, lifts the floorboard and returns with a bottle of whisky.*) Who'll have a drink? You, Mr Atkinson? Might as well! Plenty here!

Aroha: (*anguished*) Johnny! Quiet!

Johnny: Better not, though, eh Mr Atkinson? Know what happens when a Māori takes to the bottle, don't you? Goes to the pack: can't trust him. I'm sure you know that, don't you Mr Atkinson?

Atkinson: (*shouting*) Put that away! And stop talking like that! You're only doing yourself harm. Sergeant: have you finished?

Robinson: Got the money, Mrs Mataira?

She gives it to him.

I'll write you a receipt. (*He does so, at the table.*) Now you know what this means, Johnny. You're free to go where you please between now and Wednesday when you will appear in the Magistrates Court at Waikaru. If you don't turn up, your mother will lose her fifty quid. All right?

Johnny: Yes.

Johnny gives Aroha the receipt.

Atkinson: Now, Johnny. Where's Jezebel?

Johnny: Stable.

Atkinson: Right. Then I'll order the float for two, so I want you over first thing after lunch.

Aroha: You want Johnny to go on working for you? Now?

Atkinson: I can't get a boy to take his place in five minutes. And it seems I've lost Queenie too, today. Fruit still has to be picked, graded and packed. Work goes on, you know. You'd better come too, Mrs Mataira. Better be occupied at a time like this.

Aroha: Yes. You are right. We shall come.

Atkinson: (*with a sudden gruff kindliness*) Look, Mrs Mataira. It's
                  bad, but it could be worse. He hasn't killed anyone.
                  We'll all help him at the Court. Promise. Sergeant:
                  can I give you a lift?

Robinson: Thanks a lot. Cheero, Mrs Mataira. Good luck, Johnny.

                  *They go. A long silence. Aroha sinks into the chair by the
                  table. Johnny still holds the bottle.*

Aroha: Oh. God, boy. What madness got into you?

Johnny: (*in a low voice*) I couldn't stay here after what
                  happened. I had to think. So I galloped away on
                  Jezebel, miles along the beach, up the coast, until
                  I came to some rocks. And I jumped down and sat
                  on the sand. And I drank. I must have drunk half a
                  bottle.

Aroha: Why! Why do you drink?

Johnny: (*savagely*) I like the taste! It makes me feel good! Don't
                  you see, Ma! I need that, I need it! And I fell asleep
                  then, the taiaha in my hand. And I dreamed, Ma. And
                  Whetumarama came to me in my dream, shouting
                  with rage in my ears!

                  Ka whawhai, ka whawhai, e he!
                  Ka whawhai, ka whawhai, e ha!

                  Then a fire seemed to burn in me, all over me, and
                  I woke, galloped back to Te Parenga until I came to
                  the Church. I pushed the door, I went inside. There
                  he was, hanging there. The Light of the World. And
                  I thought of His love, the love that binds all wounds.
                  Well, Queenie was wounded, Ma! Did it bind her
                  wound? And I'm wounded, too! All of us: all cut off
                  and lost! If that was the light, I want no more light!
                  And I climbed up on the altar and threw the taiaha at
                  that face of lies!

Aroha cries out in anguish. Her voice trails off into a long keen.

And the glass roared and the face disappeared for ever! Dark, all dark. I had put out the Light of the World! And I shouted with joy, yes with joy, Ma.

Aroha's wail is now a thin thread of sound.

Ma. You're too big. The world can't hold you. It's too small out there. You tried to make me as big as you. I tried, Ma. But me: I'm not big. I'm just a Māori boy who wants to live in his own way, easy, quiet. I had to show you that, Ma.

She is silent now, showing him no sign.

Look at me, Ma. Look at me!

Aroha rises, stumbles round the table and picks up the taiaha, turns and slowly raises it above her head.

Aroha: Jesu! My King! My dead King! Auē!

Her long cry hangs on the air as the lights fade.

Act Three

Late afternoon, some months later. The hanging branch of the pōhutukawa is much lower on the porch.

Mrs Atkinson is on the porch, sweeping. She wears a print dress and a handkerchief round her hair. On the table are old flowers in vases and new ones, ready for trimming. The bedroom door opens and Dr Lomas enters. He carries a medical bag, round his neck a stethoscope, in his free hand a sphygmomanometer. Mrs Atkinson comes in when she sees him.

Mrs Atkinson: Well, David.

Lomas: No change.

Mrs Atkinson: Can't you put a name to it yet?

Lomas: (*taking the air out of the sphygmomanometer*) In clinical terms, nothing's the matter, Isobel. Her blood pressure's a little low and she's badly undernourished. Hardly eaten a bite in four weeks. She's slightly anaemic, but only slightly. If she started eating again, she'd be as right as a trivet. But she won't. She lies in there, hour after hour, her old Māori clothes all around her. She holds a tiki in her hand and sometimes you'd swear she was gone, but you see her finger and thumb rubbing away at it all the time.

Mrs Atkinson: She should be in hospital.

Lomas: Of course she should but she won't be moved. Well, I can't force her.

Mrs Atkinson:　But can you do nothing for her?

Lomas:　And what would you suggest? I do my best. Iron injections to create more red corpuscles, multiple vitamins and intravenous glucose to keep her pecker up. Once a day, I insist she walk around the room to keep the use of her legs. And that's the end of my road. We doctors think of a body as a machine. I know that's not strictly true but for an old hack like me, it'll serve. Well, if your machine runs down, you've got to recharge it. But if the owner of your machine doesn't want it to go, then that's the end of your mechanic. He's stymied.

Mrs Atkinson:　But there's no need for her to die!

Lomas:　Ask yourself, Isobel: is there any need for her to live?

Atkinson:　Oh, David. She's a mother: Johnny needs her. Is it because of him, all this?

Lomas:　Ay. That's part of it, no doubt.

Mrs Atkinson:　But the magistrate wasn't severe. Three months' reformative detention. You can't call that excessive. And we all spoke up for him: Clive, the Minister, you David.

Lomas:　Ay.

Mrs Atkinson:　And the way people here rallied round: it was remarkable. Restored all the damage, public subscription for the window: all she had to pay were the Court costs.

Lomas:　Ay, I know all that.

Mrs Atkinson:　What's it all about then?

Lomas:　(*sorting through his bag*) Search me. I only know this much. Her will to live has gone: the cord that holds her to life has been cut. Now when we're disappointed or upset, what happens? Do we sit down

and methodically die? Not very often. We Europeans
have worked out all sorts of little dodges to keep alive
on like neurosis and every kind of psychic disorder.
I've seen hundreds in my time. I have spots before
my eyes, doctor. The colour blue makes me nervous
doctor. I feel men are following me, doctor. And that
keeps them going. They use this rubbish to plague
the life out of their families, but they live, Isobel, they
live. But Mrs Mataira's a Māori and neurosis isn't in
her scheme. On the day her boy was taken off, a dark
shadow seemed to fall on her. Two weeks ago, she
took to her bed and she hasn't been up since except
for what I make her do. Drugs can't help her. And
ordinary decent human kindness like yours can't help
her. She's beyond our reach.

Mrs Atkinson: All I do is clean the place out and stick a few
flowers in vases. I don't expect to help her. But you're
a doctor. It's your job to make her well.

Lomas: Listen, Isobel. Forty years ago, when I first came to
Te Parenga, I saw this kind of thing. There were a
lot of Māoris here then, and though they didn't rush
about in flax skirts, they lived very much in the old
way. Well, one day a young fella came to me. He'd
broken a tapu, offended one of his atuas. Well, it's the
tohunga's job to exorcise him but the tohunga was in
gaol for running sly grog. So he comes to the Pākehā
tohunga—me—and says, Doctor: I've broken a
tapu. Help me or I die. What could I do? He was the
picture of health. So I gave him a sedative and sent
him packing. In a week, he was dead . . . See? That's
what we're up against. I sell a cure of bodies, Isobel.
What she needs now is a cure of souls. And that's
where I wave ye goodbye.

He scribbles a prescription.

And how's little Sylvia?

Mrs Atkinson: You can see for yourself next week.

Lomas: Ah! A visit?

Mrs Atkinson: She's having a baby in November.

Lomas: So she comes straight home to mother. Tell her the
glad news. Very nice, too.

Mrs Atkinson: It's good to know she still needs me a little.

Lomas: And she's happy there?

Mrs Atkinson: Why on earth shouldn't she be? A husband who
dotes on her, lovely house, two Māori girls to help her
run it, siesta from two till five, gin and tonic at six,
dinner at seven.

Lomas: Lucky girl.

Mrs Atkinson: That's what I tell her. If ever there was a girl cut out
for an easy life, it's that girl.

Lomas: Here's a repeat of those tablets. She's enough to last
the night but ye'd better get more tomorrow.

Mrs Atkinson takes it and nods.

Ye look tired, Isobel. How many nights is it now?

Mrs Atkinson: Six in a row. Clive's getting awfully fed up.

Lomas: Tonight, too?

Mrs Atkinson: No, thank goodness. Mr Sedgwick will be back.
He's been away for a few days. We'd been taking it
night about, sleeping here . . . Queenie's bed is full of
lumps.

Lomas: You're a good woman, Isobel.

Mrs Atkinson: It's the least I can do.

Footsteps.

Lomas: (*looking out*) Ah, it's your relief. The soul-curer. Watch
that tree, Vicar. Duck.

Sedgwick comes in.

Well, Vicar.

Sedgwick: Any change?

Lomas: None. Neither forward nor back, not up, not down.

Sedgwick: Well, I've brought something that may just tip the scale.

Mrs Atkinson: What?

Sedgwick: Johnny.

Mrs Atkinson: Johnny? But hasn't he another three weeks to go?

Sedgwick: Yes. But I've been to the reformatory. Spoke to the superintendent, told him about Mrs Mataira and the background of the case. Result: Johnny's free.

Mrs Atkinson: Where is he?

Sedgwick: At my house. He'll be down in fifteen minutes. I thought we'd better prepare her first.

Lomas: Ah. Quite right. Then I have a few instructions. (*He opens the door, disappears for a moment, and returns.*) She's sleeping now. She'll wake in half an hour or so. Whatever happens, this mustn't be sprung on her. Snuff out like a taper in her low state. You'd better wait here until she wakes, then one of you warn her. Who's it to be? You, Isobel?

Mrs Atkinson: Yes, if I'm here. If I'm not, Mr Sedgwick will tell her.

Lomas: Ye know: I'm greatly relieved. Oh, quite selfish: just for myself. At my age, ye don't welcome finality. When she goes, it'll be the end of an era at Te Parenga. Which would remind me of the end of my own. Well, if she rallies at all, it'll be for the boy, I'm sure of that. Very pleased. Very relieved. I'll be in tomorrow, I feel more hopeful. Goodnight to ye both. (*He goes onto the porch, bends to avoid the hanging branch of the* *pōhutukawa*.) Tell Johnny his first job's to cut back the pohute. It's a menace all over the porch like this. Have to cut my way in, soon . . . So long. (*He goes.*)

Sedgwick: Can I help.

Mrs Atkinson: No, really. I'm only filling in time until Clive comes for me . . . Tell me: how is Johnny?

Sedgwick: A quite remarkable change. He's a man, now.

Mrs Atkinson: He needed to grow up.

Sedgwick: He did it a hard way, but he'll be none the worse off in the long run. Something had to happen here: something had to break. He's a fine lad. Be a great credit to his race. They were very impressed in Tamatea.

Mrs Atkinson: Tamatea? He's been there?

Sedgwick: Yes, we went together.

Mrs Atkinson: You? So that's where you've been! Why didn't you tell me?

Sedgwick: I didn't want to raise any false hopes.

Mrs Atkinson: Then you've seen Queenie. How is she?

Sedgwick: I was just in time to give her away.

Mrs Atkinson: Queenie, married?

Sedgwick: Yes, all in white, with a crown. I waived my scruples. They didn't seem to matter down there.

Mrs Atkinson: So she got her wish at last. And the man didn't mind?

Sedgwick: Oh no. Only a young chap: twenty-six, twenty-seven. But his wife died last year in childbirth. Queenie's taken over his five children to say nothing of her own in November.

Mrs Atkinson: Oh my goodness. She'll be busy.

Sedgwick: Well, she'll have plenty of help. She's got the tribe at her feet. Really come into her own. Her wedding was the biggest party there for years.

Mrs Atkinson: What are they really like, the Ngāti-Raukura?

Sedgwick: From what Mrs Mataira said, I was prepared for anything. Vice, squalor, and an odour of decay. Well, I found no refinements. They've got about thirty acres and I suppose there are fifty houses. Nothing special about any of them, nothing to say Māori to you—just houses. But the life there! They seem to laugh all day long. They gave me a wonderful welcome—I've still got indigestion from the hāngī—is that what you call it? Mutton bird, wrapped in leaves and cooked on hot stones. Greasy! You can imagine what it did to my clerical serge. Well, there I sat, chewing away, with the day exploding into the most gorgeous sunset I've ever seen and half a dozen young chaps in T-shirts and jeans singing songs and playing the guitar. I don't think I've ever been so happy in my life.

Mrs Atkinson: And Johnny? Did he fit in?

Sedgwick: A little awkward at first. But the boys kidded him along a bit: he kidded back. They showed him a few chords on the guitar. After a couple of days, he was completely at home . . . She's been so wrong!

Mrs Atkinson: Mrs Mataira?

Sedgwick: To hear her talk, you would have thought her tribe was derelict. Well, there's a certain slackness there, I'll grant her that. Their market gardens will never win prizes, there are no lace curtains at the windows and the paternity of the children isn't always foolproof. But there's such life there, such joy in simple things, so much music and laughter, such a fine distaste for those nagging things that make us so miserable: time, security, money. I tell you I found more true religion there, more real simplicity of spirit than anywhere I've been here. For a dispossessed race, they're wonderfully cheerful.

Mrs Atkinson: And what was all this for, Mr Sedgwick?

Sedgwick: Can't you guess? To try and settle the Matairas at Tamatea, where they should have been years ago. I took Johnny along to test him: he passed. As for Queenie, she might have been there all her life.

Mrs Atkinson: And Aroha? How would they receive her?

Sedgwick: Like a queen. They want the past: they want her authority, her majesty. And they want it now. So they've given me an embassy. I'm to sell her land as soon as possible; Johnny's here to fortify her and two of her cousins are on their way now to look after her until she can travel.

Mrs Atkinson: How splendid. You've been wonderful, Mr Sedgwick. But—will she go?

Sedgwick: She'll have to. It's her only hope now.

A pause.

Mrs Atkinson: (*diffidently*) Is this your first parish?

Sedgwick: Yes.

Mrs Atkinson: But you're not—

Sedgwick: No. I'm thirty-eight.

Mrs Atkinson: Do you mind my asking: what brought you to the Church?

Sedgwick: (*after a pause*) Call it a moment of insight.

Mrs Atkinson: You were in the war, I heard.

Sedgwick: Oh, yes. I played my part, like the rest of my generation, in mass murder. Suddenly this moment. I knew that love is not just a soiled word. So: here I am.

Mrs Atkinson: And why here?

Sedgwick: A fresh start. A young country. One feeds oneself on such illusions.

Mrs Atkinson: (*stopping her work*) I wish I could feel some of these things. I've tried. But I can't pray. I feel a fool on my knees, and God Almighty and Omnipotent: I can't believe it. Do you know the only time I've ever felt religion as a deep—what do you say—spiritual force?

Sedgwick: When?

Mrs Atkinson: Years ago. I was next to Mrs Mataira at communion. Here is My Body, here is My Blood—just words to me, just a tasteless wafer and insipid wine. But from her, I felt it wash over me like a wave; I could somehow see the bread and wine turning to flesh and blood. And this was for Christ, for my God. We'd destroyed hers. It seemed all wrong.

Sedgwick: Do you think Mrs Mataira is a Christian?

Mrs Atkinson: She puts me to shame.

Sedgwick: 'I live, yet not I, but Christ in me.' Is that Mrs Mataira?

Mrs Atkinson: I tell you, I could see the Word turning to flesh and blood.

Sedgwick: You were just awed by her intensity. For us, whose feelings are—what shall I say—set low, anything at high pitch makes us feel inadequate. But don't assume from that that she's a Christian. That pride, that sense of honour, that forces her to commit terrible injustice, inflict on herself the greatest humiliations—

Mrs Atkinson: (*amazed*) Can this be Mrs Mataira you're talking about?

Sedgwick: No other. Poor creature: she's a battlefield. Christ and Whetumarama. She has seen his star in the East—do you know what Whetumarama means?

Mrs Atkinson: I don't know a word of Māori.

Sedgwick: It means shining star. Look up there, on her wall. The Light of the World and the shining star. Which star? Sometimes one, sometimes the other. They've fused in her mind, until she doesn't know where the light comes from.

Mrs Atkinson: You make her sound so small . . .

Sedgwick: Oh no, no. Don't mistake me. She's got size, grandeur. We're little people, you and I. She's from a forgotten race. But you can't live on that scale any more. She tried: there was grandeur in her attempt. But her children wrecked it, as they had to. And if she's to go on living in the little world, then she'll have to cut herself down to fit it.

Mrs Atkinson: Will she do that?

Sedgwick: I'm counting on Johnny.

Mrs Atkinson: (*rising*) Why should she cut herself down to size? She's got immense nobility. If she's not that, she's nothing. Who'd want to be my size, sitting here, cutting flowers? For nearly twenty years I patronised her; thought of her almost as a servant. Do you remember her at Sylvia's wedding? She made us all look like pigs at their troughs. I never saw her; I never wanted to see her as she is. And when it comes to a crisis, what do I do? Snip flowers. Pathetic, isn't it?

Sedgwick: We can only offer what's in us.

Mrs Atkinson: Beside her, I'm nothing. Nothing. Excuse me.

She goes out quickly to the tap. A pause. Clive Atkinson walks onto the porch. His hat is removed by the overhanging branch.

Atkinson: Damn that thing! I've told her time and again to cut it down. Ah, what does it matter now, anyway. (*Entering*) Hello, Sedgwick. Where's my wife?

Sedgwick: She went out to the tap. Back in a minute.

Atkinson: Do I look excited?

Sedgwick: Yes, you do. What's up?

Atkinson: Tell you in a minute. Isobel?

Mrs Atkinson: (*off*) Coming Clive. (*She appears.*)

Atkinson: What's the matter?

Mrs Atkinson: If you must know, I've been crying.

Atkinson: What about?

Mrs Atkinson: Things.

Atkinson: Well, dry your eyes, because I've got news for you . . . How would you like to have twelve thousand pounds?

Mrs Atkinson: What do you mean?

Atkinson: I've spent the whole day with Claude Johnson— you remember him, Sedgwick—spoke at Sylvia's wedding—land agent. If I can get hold of this piece here, there's a syndicate that'll take the whole sixty acres as a housing estate. Twelve thousand smackers in cash.

Mrs Atkinson: But Clive! Your family's been here for seventy five years!

Atkinson: I know, dear, I know. It's been a wrench, I can tell you. When you think of all that the Atkinsons have done for Te Parenga! No, it wasn't easy. But once I made up my mind, I was free. Free as air. Now the important thing is: will Mrs Mataira sell?

Mrs Atkinson: She's in no position to sell or even to think about it. She's frail and ill.

Atkinson: But I met old Lomas. He says there's nothing wrong with her.

Mrs Atkinson: Take a look at her, then.

Atkinson: Look, I've got to clinch this thing in the next few days or they won't play. Oh, don't look at me like that, Isobel! The orchard's gone to rack and ruin! Grass a foot high, grapefruit falling off the trees. Once the Matairas left, I was sunk. Damn it, they *were* the orchard! And I can't get anyone else to stay here. We're going downhill fast, Isobel, and I'm being worked to a frazzle. Sell: that's the thing, isn't it? You can see the sense of that, surely?

Mrs Atkinson: I'll tell you what I can see, Clive. A sick, stricken woman. And I can see a certain fitness and respect that you're not showing her. As it happens, Mr Sedgwick's just come back from Tamatea with instructions to sell the land for the tribe. So it's quite likely that Mrs Mataira may want to sell. Johnny's here, too; we expect him any minute. But you don't make a sale now, Clive.

Atkinson: Well, why didn't you say so before? Listen, Sedgwick: tell her I'll give a thousand pounds for her land.

Mrs Atkinson: (*raising her voice*) Clive: go away. I will not have haggling in this house at this time. You've no place here but to offer your respect. Talk about it when she's well but not now, Clive, do you understand? Not now!

The door is thrown open and Aroha stands there. Her face is gaunt and ravaged and her long hair hangs in two dishevelled plaits. Over her nightdress she wears a Māori blanket; from one ear hangs a long greenstone pendant, round her neck a tiki.

Aroha: (*thickly*) What are you doing here? Get out! Get out of my house!

They do not move for a moment, shocked.

Mrs Atkinson: I was just brightening the place up a little, a few flowers . . .

Aroha stumbles over to one of the vases, grabs a bunch and hurls it to the floor.

Aroha: Get out! Get out!

Atkinson: Now wait a minute. This won't get us anywhere!

Mrs Atkinson: Quiet, Clive . . . Mrs Mataira: there is something I have to tell you . . .

Aroha turns on her a look so baleful that Mrs Atkinson cowers.

Mrs Mataira . . .

Johnny's call is heard, long and melancholy. Aroha freezes. He appears on the porch, neatly dressed, carrying a small suitcase. He leaves it at the door and goes to Aroha.

Johnny: Ma.

She gives him a long look. He takes her hand and presses it to his cheek, then leads her gently to the sofa and helps her onto it.

Mrs Atkinson: Hello, Johnny. Mr Sedgwick's told me. I think it's fine. But your mother's really very ill. Dr Lomas comes every day, but she'll need all your care, too. If there is anything I can do, you've only to let me know.

Johnny nods. Atkinson comes up to him, shakes his hand.

Atkinson: Hello, Johnny. Good to see you back. Wouldn't recognise the orchard. Proper mess now, without you running it . . . Johnny, I know this isn't the best time to broach the subject, but I'm selling the orchard and I'll need this piece too, to make the sale worthwhile. Could you ask your mother if—

Mrs Atkinson: (*swiftly*) Whatever happens, Johnny, you mustn't think of anything just now but getting your mother well. And of course, you must stay here just as long as you need.

Atkinson: What do you think you're doing, Isobel?

Mrs Atkinson: I know what I'm doing.

Aroha: (*faintly*) Johnny.

He bends his head and she whispers to him. Johnny walks to the door.

Johnny: Will you all go now, please.

Sedgwick: (*moving out*) Yes, of course. You know where to find me, Johnny.

Atkinson looks at Johnny, is about to speak, then goes, quickly. Mrs Atkinson moves towards the sofa.

Mrs Atkinson: Mrs Mataira . . .

Aroha sits like stone.

Atkinson: (*off*) Come on, Isobel! You're wasting your time.

Mrs Atkinson goes. Johnny rushes to Aroha, kneels beside her.

Johnny: Ma! I missed you, Ma! Why are you so ill? I'm home now, Ma. I'll look after you. Get well, Ma, and we'll go to Tamatea. Sell the land and we'll go where we belong. They're waiting for you, Ma. I've been there and they all want you to come. You'll be the big boss: keep them all in order . . . Ma. Speak to me, Ma.

Aroha: Get out, Johnny. Go. Go away.

Johnny's eyes widen in terror.

Get out, Johnny.

Johnny: (*anguished*) Ma!

His head falls in her lap. She looks down at it, then lifts it and looks into his eyes.

Aroha: Ka tō he rā: Ka ura he rā.

Johnny: (*translating slowly*) 'A sun sets: a sun rises.'

*Aroha nods, Johnny understands. He looks at her, rises
and finds his suitcase. He stands a moment by the door,
looking at her. Then runs out. Aroha rises painfully,
moves to the mantelpiece, looks gravely at the pictures,
then takes the taiaha and turns back towards the table.
Sedgwick appears on the porch. They look at each other.*

Sedgwick: Why?

Aroha: He came too soon. He shall not see me die.

Sedgwick: No one can tell the hour of death.

Aroha: I have willed it. (*She moves on towards the table, sits.*)

Sedgwick: But, why!

Aroha: Who lives by the sword shall die by the sword.

Sedgwick: What do you mean?

Aroha: Your cross, a sword. To cut my people down. The
Light of the World, no light, Only dark, dark,
dark. What has your Christ brought me! Affliction.
Disgrace. Shame.

Sedgwick: Then offer Him your shame. Think of Him on the
Cross, naked and mocked. Think of that shame, then
of yours . . .

Aroha: I gave Him my whole life. I made His pain my own.
The thorns. The nails. The wounded side. I ate His
flesh. I drank His blood. What more does He want?

Sedgwick: You, Aroha.

Aroha: He cheated me!

Sedgwick: (*gently*) No, Aroha. You cheated Him.

A pause.

Aroha: How?

Sedgwick: By pride. Your Christ had the face of a Māori chief.
Was it love he counselled? No. Pride, pride. This land of

yours, a green pocket in a conquered land, a sanctuary
to pride. From pride you built a world for your children
out of the air; no wonder it would not hold them.

Aroha: Must your Christ have everything, then?

Sedgwick: Everything. Strip yourself of pride, honour, dignity
and respect. Find them again in Him. Live, Aroha.

Aroha: Live. Live! How shall I live! You want me to go to
Tamatea; grow fat and swing pois. You want to see my
race a lot of laughing clowns and I an old clown with
them. I will not. I will not!

Sedgwick: Clown? Never. Mother; leader of your people—there's
your path. Everything pulls you to Tamatea. Johnny,
Queenie. Not even this land will remain in your
hands. Accept the Pākehā's conquest by time. Forget
greatness: forget history. Find harmony and a lasting
peace.

Aroha: Is that my choice, then?

Sedgwick: Yes.

Aroha: On your honour and your faith?

Sedgwick: On my honour and my faith.

Aroha: (*rising slowly*) Then, on *my* honour, I choose. I choose
if it must be, the way of pride. I will go proud down
to my death, for that is all I have left. I will not be
humbled, I will die true to my past. No, not even for
Him will I weaken; I will not carve up my life, slice
by slice from the whale. I go to Whetumarama and
the gods of my people. That is my choice. That is my
victory. (*She sinks, exhausted.*)

Sedgwick: There will be no victory in that death.

Aroha: I go to dark. To my only home.

Sedgwick: Then I can do nothing more for you.

She does not reply. He touches her lightly on the shoulder.

I shall pray for your soul, Aroha. (*He goes, closing the door softly.*)

Aroha: (*faintly*) Ka tō he rā: ka ura he rā.

Her head falls onto her breast. The faint throbbing of a Māori chant. The door opens. Two Māori women stand there, dressed in black, black scarves over their heads. They move in cautiously, one on each side of Aroha, exchange a glance, and close in. One of them touches Aroha on the cheek. A long wail. 'AUĒ!'

New Zealand Playscripts

General Editor: John Thomson